# 5-MINUTE BIBLE STUDIES

*for*

# *Women*

Naomi Schmidt
Editor

NORTHWESTERN PUBLISHING HOUSE
Milwaukee, Wisconsin

Northwestern Publishing House
N16W23379 Stone Ridge Dr., Waukesha WI 53188-1108
www.nph.net

Published 2025
Printed in the United States of America
ISBN 978-0-8100-3321-4
ISBN 978-0-8100-3322-1 (e-book)

25 26 27 28 29 30 31 32 33 34 10 9 8 7 6 5 4 3 2 1

# Preface

❖

Life lessons are often learned through momentary glimpses that help us see our life and faith more clearly. I caught such illuminating glimpses years ago when I met Adela Spaude at a pregnancy counseling center in Watertown, Wisconsin. I heard her weave stories from the life of Christ into discussions with women who needed hope in difficult situations. Those glimpses of the way she listened and responded with gentleness were a tremendous influence. Adela always found a way to talk about Jesus and his forgiveness. She knew Jesus so well and took every opportunity to share his grace. Her understanding of the accounts of Jesus' life opened doors to talk about his saving work.

More recently, I heard Martin Luther College professor Mark Paustian encourage women to learn five Bible accounts they could tell in two minutes. He said, "Think about who needs to hear that story." Imagine how people could relate to the dynamic accounts of the prodigal son, the woman at the well, or the Pharisee and the tax collector.

What great encouragement to study the gospels!

I was compelled to study Luke's account. The gentle physician investigated Christ's life and recorded it with Spirit-led words. In the brief studies in this book, Luke's words encourage readers to learn what Jesus did. Learn who he is. Think about how *you* need to hear each story. *Keep* thinking about it as God works it into your heart and mind. It will be there at just the right time to shine with love and truth that give others hope and encouragement.

May the glimpses of Jesus' love and grace that you see in this book strengthen your faith and fuel you with pure nourishment for your soul and mind. May the questions and prayers linger in your thoughts and help you see opportunities to share God's grace with others.

Jesus walks with you every day. Take his hand for a few minutes and listen to the story of his life.

Naomi Schmidt, Editor

## List of Authors

**Emma Hayes**
St. John's on the Hillside Lutheran Church, Milwaukee, Wisconsin

**Samantha King**
Divine Savior Lutheran Church, Celina, Texas

**Emily Krill**
St. Paul's Lutheran Church, Muskego, Wisconsin

**Katie Martin**
St. John's Lutheran Church, Jefferson, Wisconsin

**Angie Molkentin**
Morning Star Lutheran Church, Jackson, Wisconsin

**Naomi Schmidt**
Redeemer Lutheran Church, Fond du Lac, Wisconsin

**Dawn Schulz**
Divine Savior Lutheran Church, Delray Beach, Florida

**Holly Schwefel**
Redeemer Lutheran Church, Fond du Lac, Wisconsin

**Marilyn Sievert**
Good Shepherd Lutheran Church, West Bend, Wisconsin

**DeLyn Wagenknecht**
King of Kings Lutheran Church, Maitland, Florida

**Jes Woller**
St. John's Lutheran Church, Watertown, Wisconsin

## Table of Contents

❖

**The Orderly Account** . . . . . . . . . . . . . . . . . . . . . . . 7

**God Sets the Stage:** Luke chapter 1. . . . . . . . . . . . . . . . . . . 9

**Meet the Christ Child:** Luke chapter 2 . . . . . . . . . . . . . . . . 15

**His Ministry Begins:** Luke chapters 3–4 . . . . . . . . . . . . . . . 27

**The Early Years:** Luke chapters 4–5. . . . . . . . . . . . . . . . . . 39

**Jesus Gains Popularity:** Luke chapters 6–8 . . . . . . . . . . . . . 53

**Jesus Faces Opposition:** Luke chapters 9–11 . . . . . . . . . . . . 67

**Back to Jesus' Popularity:** Luke chapter 11 . . . . . . . . . . . . . 89

**Jesus' Final Months:** Luke chapters 12–18 . . . . . . . . . . . . . . 95

**He Completes Our Salvation:** Luke chapters 18–24 . . . . . .135

**Index** . . . . . . . . . . . . . . . . . . . . . . . . . . . . . . . . . .184

# Unfolding the Elaborate Plan

**Since I myself have carefully investigated everything from the beginning, I too decided to write an orderly account for you . . . so that you may know the certainty of the things you have been taught.**

LUKE 1:3-4 NIV

Have you ever watched a movie about an elaborate heist? A seemingly impossible plan is carried out through a fun and complex series of events and personalities. For weeks you see different people obtaining the right job, item, uniform, or relationship so they can play their specific parts. The day finally comes, and countless details are set in place to accomplish the impossible.

Rescuing our wretched souls for eternal salvation should have been an impossible plan. Yet in all of God's wisdom, he put everything into place. Scripture provides an orderly account of how God safeguarded the line of David, inspired and fulfilled prophecies hundreds of years apart, and called countless people to play their specific roles in his design for divine deliverance.

As we examine our own lives and decipher the orderly account of God's artistry and grace, we delight in the miraculous details of Jesus' life. This orderly account shows how God's plan for the salvation of our souls comes together—the impossible made possible.

- How have you seen God's hand at work in your own life?
- Who might benefit from your personal, orderly account or testimony of God's presence?

Prayer Prompt: Ask God to strengthen your trust in his design and presence in your life.

# GOD SETS THE STAGE

## *Luke chapter 1*

# GOD SETS THE STAGE

Luke chapter 1

*Lord God, you knew we needed a Savior, and in your great mercy, you shaped history to set the stage for your Son to be born. What a loving, marvelous, and intricate plan—what a gracious God you are! Thank you for your plan of salvation in Christ. Amen.*

# Prophet of the Most High

❖

**"Your wife Elizabeth will bear you a son, and you are to call him John. He will be a joy and delight to you, and many will rejoice because of his birth."**

LUKE 1:13-14 NIV

In the months before Jesus' birth, God knit together his greatest prophet in the womb of an old woman. Elizabeth and Zechariah had been childless until the angel Gabriel's unexpected announcement to Zechariah in the temple foretelling the birth of their son, John.

John would prepare the people of Israel for their long-awaited Messiah. He would break hearts with God's law and bind them up again with God's promise of forgiveness. He would speak with boldness, baptize with water, and point people to their Lord.

John was set apart for God even before his conception. He received a name from God, clear instruction for his ministry, and a soul that was filled with the Holy Spirit.

John would be the prophet of the Most High, a joy to his parents, and great in the sight of the Lord. After thousands upon thousands of years of waiting, the forerunner was being prepared to announce the coming of the Savior.

- What might Elizabeth have felt about this unexpected blessing?
- How is your life different knowing that you also have been chosen by God from before you were born?

Prayer Prompt: Ask God to help you prepare the hearts of others for the Savior who has loved them from eternity.

# Son of the Most High

**In the sixth month of Elizabeth's pregnancy, God sent the angel Gabriel to Nazareth, a town in Galilee, to a virgin. . . . The virgin's name was Mary. "You will conceive and give birth to a son, and you are to call him Jesus. He will be great and will be called the Son of the Most High."**

LUKE 1:26-27,31-32 NIV

The time had come. Everything was in place. God had been silent for hundreds of years, but now his angel Gabriel was delivering news the people of Israel had been waiting for since ancient times. The earth-shattering message fell on the ears of a young woman.

Mary, a virgin, learned she was *miraculously* about to become a mother, yet the baby in her womb would be like no other. He would be God himself, the Son of the Most High, Jesus.

Mary was given the honor of being the first person to hear the name of the promised Savior. Parents are given the authority to name their babies, and Mary would be his mother, but God named his Son. The Son of God, having all authority in heaven and on earth, would humble himself to become the sacrificial Lamb that redeemed all people. The Most High would become the least of all, and through his birth, the world would be changed forever. God's grace would be free to all people. The debt of sin will soon be paid.

- In this announcement, how did God display his love for all people?
- When you hear the name "Son of the Most High," what do you envision?

Prayer Prompt: Thank God for the gift of Jesus.

# May Your Word Be Fulfilled

**"I am the Lord's servant," Mary answered.**
**"May your word to me be fulfilled."**
**Then the angel left her.**

LUKE 1:38 NIV

As Mary took in the incredible news, her mind must have been racing with many thoughts all at once. She was speaking with an angel. The angel knew her name. She was going to be a mother. She was going to give birth to the long-promised Savior.

This was a heavy message.

God was now revealing his plan of salvation to a young woman thousands of years after he gave the first promise. Mary didn't have any status in society. How would he make this come about? She wasn't even married yet!

Mary absorbed all this news very quickly, and while she questioned how it would come to be, she didn't do so out of doubt. She trusted that God would accomplish what he said, but she also knew what it meant: in her small town of Nazareth, the gossip would characterize her as an unwed mother and Jesus as an illegitimate child. Despite responding with faith and grace, Mary's tone was hushed.

- What emotions might Mary have experienced in these moments with Gabriel?
- What might Mary have known about God's promise of the Messiah?

Prayer Prompt: Ask God to give you a heart like Mary: questioning to understand, willing to surrender control, and continually filled with grace to trust in a future unknown.

# My Spirit Rejoices

**Mary said: "My soul glorifies the Lord and my spirit rejoices in God my Savior."**
LUKE 1:46-47 NIV

Before the angel Gabriel left Mary, he told her about her cousin Elizabeth's pregnancy. Mary then hurried to the hill country, her mind certainly mulling over all that the angel had told her. As she greeted Elizabeth, the unborn John leaped in Elizabeth's womb as he came into the presence of his Savior, six months his junior and yet the "Alpha and the Omega, the First and the Last, the Beginning and the End" (Revelation 22:13).

At John's reaction, Elizabeth proclaimed her elation that God had shown Mary his favor. She praised the Lord for fulfilling his promises and sending the Messiah. Elizabeth rejoiced for all the blessings that would come from the child Mary was carrying.

In this joyous moment of fellowship with a sister in faith, Mary's heart exploded with gratitude for all that had been revealed. Mary proclaimed that the child in her womb was where mercy and might would meet. She burst forth with a song, praising God for doing great things and helping his humbled people. Her spirit glorified her Savior, the very babe growing within her.

- How has fellowship with your sisters in Christ fortified your faith life?
- Aside from worship, how do Christians glorify the Lord and rejoice in God together?

Prayer Prompt: Praise God for the blessing of Christian relationships and ask him to be glorified in your fellowship with other believers. Ask God to help you always rejoice in your Savior.

# MEET THE CHRIST CHILD

## *Luke chapter 2*

# MEET THE CHRIST CHILD

Luke chapter 2

*Holy Christ Child, in the early months of your life, it was revealed to lowly, humble people that you are the Savior of the world. May we always revere you as the Lord who saves us from our sin. What a joy to meet you in the Word! Amen.*

# Enter, King Jesus!

**In those days Caesar Augustus issued a decree that a census should be taken.**

LUKE 2:1 NIV

In response to Caesar's decree, Joseph went from Nazareth to Judea to register with Mary, who was expecting a child. While they were there, she gave birth to a son and placed him in a manger. In eternity, God planned for Jesus to be born into the Roman world. A self-proclaimed victor, Caesar Augustus hailed himself as a prince of peace, establishing the *Pax Romana,* or "Roman peace." Taxation provided better travel on roads lined with statues proclaiming, "Caesar is Lord." But his rule was evil—he murdered and suppressed his opposition.

Enter, King Jesus! While Caesar Augustus literally paved the way, the true Prince of Peace is the way. No darkness thrives in his kingdom because "the LORD has anointed [Jesus] to preach good news to the afflicted" (Isaiah 61:1 EHV). God's salvation had come!

Yet Jesus was shunned. Though he deserved a palace, he was born in a cave meant for animals. Sadly, the pivotal point of history was missed by all but Mary, Joseph, and some shepherds. Yet God knew what he was doing to ensure the world's redemption.

- Compare Caesar's rule to Isaiah's prophecy about Jesus.
- Where in your life has God's way been higher than yours?

Prayer Prompt: Ask God to calm your fears as the world grows darker.

# The Most Unique Announcement

**There were shepherds living out in the fields nearby, keeping watch over their flocks at night. An angel of the Lord appeared to them, and the glory of the Lord shone around them, and they were terrified. But the angel said to them, "Do not be afraid. I bring you good news that will cause great joy for all the people. Today . . . a Savior has been born."**

LUKE 2:8-11 NIV

Most birth announcements are filled with cute words like "Hello, little one" or the baby's name scrawled in large letters. But this very unique birth message will never ever be topped anywhere, anytime—not ever again. The King of heaven came down, and his glory broke loose.

Stunning light shattered the black night! Though terrified, the shepherds watched and waited. Next, an angel spoke directly to them: "Do not be afraid." Familiar words from God—first spoken to Abraham, Moses, and others—now rang in their ears, calming their fears.

"I bring you good news. It will bring great joy for all the people. Today in the town of David a Savior has been born to you. He is the Messiah, the Lord" (Luke 2:10-11 NIRV).

- What words in Jesus' birth announcement bring you "great joy"?
- Why do angels often say, "Do not be afraid"?

Prayer Prompt: Praise God for shattering the darkness of your sin with his good news of a Savior.

# Seek and Find

**"Today in the town of David a Savior has been born to you. . . . This will be a sign to you: You will find a baby wrapped in cloths and lying in a manger."**

LUKE 2:11-12 NIV

Many people like games with clues given to find the answer. Do you think God likes them also, since he placed several tips in these verses?

"The town of David"—King David's little burg of Bethlehem. "A sign"—look to see this! "You will find"—yes, go and leave the sheep. "A baby wrapped in cloths"—the original word for *cloths* also referred to cloth strips used for wrapping the legs of newborn lambs. "Lying in a manger"—a newborn laid in a feeding trough.

I wonder if the night air could have carried the baby's first cry to the shepherds' campfire. Could the place where Jesus was born be known as a birthing place for lambs?

While God left out some of those details, we do know these shepherds had enough courage, confidence, and clues to seek and find the treasure their weary hearts desired. Can there be any doubt? God thought of every little thing as he put his plan into place.

- Why is it so like God to give the full address of Jesus' birth with hints and clues?
- What details of Christ's birth do you wonder about?

Prayer Prompt: Thank God for the hundreds of promises in the Bible that help us seek and find him.

# A Great Company

**Suddenly a great company of the heavenly host appeared with the angel, praising God and saying, "Glory to God in the highest heaven, and on earth peace to those on whom his favor rests." When the angels had left them and gone into heaven, the shepherds said to one another, "Let's go to Bethlehem and see this thing that has happened, which the Lord has told us about."**

LUKE 2:13-15 NIV

As the Christmas account progresses, are you getting a sense of the dignified, exuberant atmosphere and celebration? Bright lights, announcements, and a game of seek and find. What next?

Luke continues with urgency. A luminous cloud of angels hovers in the sky. Praising God, they spoke words that will be caroled for centuries: Glory to God! Peace on earth! Songs of joy, gladness, peace, and wonder! Good news for all!

When the worship ended, the awestruck shepherds could not wait to see what had happened. Why did they believe? Because of the light show or the angels?

Neither of these.

It was the Word of God. They left to see what "the Lord [had] told [them] about." Like the shepherds, we can believe and not doubt. God keeps his word. His promises are sure.

The baby in the manger does not disappoint! The Messiah is the answer.

- Which is your favorite carol containing the angels' words?
- How does the favor of God rest on you?

Prayer Prompt: Praise God by singing or playing a Christmas carol.

**Simeon took him in his arms and praised God, saying: "For my eyes have seen your salvation, which you have prepared in the sight of all nations: a light for revelation to the Gentiles, and the glory of your people Israel."**

LUKE 2:28,30-32 NIV

Moved by the Spirit, a man named Simeon went to the temple the same day Mary and Joseph brought Jesus to be consecrated to the Lord. The Spirit had revealed to Simeon that he would not die before his eyes had seen the promised Savior.

As the new parents navigated the temple gates, most people simply saw a young couple carrying a tiny baby and a meager offering. Simeon, however, was given insight to see so much more.

Through eyes of faith, Simeon saw prophecies fulfilled. In human flesh, he witnessed God's long-promised Messiah. He gazed on the salvation of the nations. He saw the one who would reveal God's mercy to the Gentiles. He held the Redeemer, the Savior who would pay for all the sins of the world.

With praise and gratitude for God's faithfulness, Simeon knew the desire of his heart had come. The promised Messiah was in his arms, and his soul was at peace.

- How does Simeon's story strengthen you as you wait to see Jesus?
- Have you ever gazed into a newborn's face and wondered what the future might bring?

Prayer Prompt: Praise Jesus by filling in the blank: "Jesus, you are ________."

# A Sword Will Pierce Your Own Soul

**"This child is destined to cause the falling and rising of many in Israel, and to be a sign that will be spoken against, so that the thoughts of many hearts will be revealed. And a sword will pierce your own soul too."**

LUKE 2:34-35 NIV

Simeon embraced the fulfillment of prophecy in his arms, and by the Spirit he also spoke words of prophecy. The seemingly ordinary child he held would alter the course of world history. This humble infant would one day, and for all time, cause many to stumble and fall over his teachings while becoming salvation for a multitude of others.

As Mary entered the temple with ceremonial offerings for purification, she held the baby boy who would become the sacrifice to end all sacrifices. One day, Mary's own soul would be pierced as she'd helplessly witness the deep, soul-crushing anguish of her dying son and Savior. The sword of suffering that would cut down her son would also pierce her own soul.

In these words, Mary was warned how Jesus would be treated by his own people. Even as a baby, Jesus was revealed as the Suffering Servant of God.

- Some stumble and fall over Jesus' teachings, but how do his teachings cause believers to rise?
- How has faith in Jesus been a blessing to you?

Prayer Prompt: Confess the times when you have stumbled over Jesus' teachings. Thank Jesus for being the sacrifice that paid for your sin.

# A Godly Widow

**Coming up to them at that very moment,
[Anna] gave thanks to God and spoke about the child
to all who were looking forward to
the redemption of Jerusalem.**

LUKE 2:38 NIV

Anna was an 84-year-old widow who never left the temple, fasting and praying both day and night. She was a Jewish woman who had lost her husband early in life, after only seven years of marriage. Without a husband to provide for her, life would have been difficult for Anna. Yet God had blessed her with the ability to know and interpret his Word and to understand his will.

Anna believed a Redeemer would come, not with political ambition but as a ransom for sin. At the very moment Simeon was bearing witness to the Redeemer's arrival, Anna was also praising God for the Savior's birth.

Anna knew firsthand the meaning of the sacrifices offered at the temple. She understood that a sacrifice—a ransom—was needed to redeem Israel. This ransom meant the shedding of blood and the taking of life to pay for sin. Jesus was the ransom. As she admired the baby Jesus, she knew what his future would bring and told those waiting for the Messiah that he had come.

- What sights, sounds, and smells would Anna have witnessed in the temple?
- How will it feel to gaze upon the face of your Savior?

Prayer Prompt: Praise God for the perfect life, innocent death, and glorious resurrection of your Redeemer!

# Letting Go

**"Why were you searching for me?" [Jesus] asked.**
**"Didn't you know I had to be in my Father's house?"**
**Then he went down to Nazareth with them. . . .**
**But his mother treasured all these things in her heart.**

LUKE 2:49,51 NIV

Jesus and his parents celebrated the Passover in Jerusalem. When it was over, Jesus stayed behind in the temple to take his seat among the most learned men in Jerusalem. They were amazed at his understanding of Scripture and his answers to their questions.

As his parents traveled back to Nazareth, they realized he was missing. They backtracked, searched, and found him in the temple. They too were astonished at what they saw.

It was a sinless rebuke that Jesus gave his mother and in that moment, she pondered the special child she had been chosen to raise, just as she had done at his birth. She knew his purpose was to complete God's plan of salvation for sinners.

So it began.

A Jewish boy took his place in the religious community. A Savior paved the way of salvation. And a mother realized the necessity of letting her little boy grow up.

- What do you think Mary treasured in her heart as she took in the scene at the temple?
- Was there ever a time when you realized it was time to let go?

Prayer Prompt: Ask Jesus to show you places where you can let go to make room for his will in your life.

# Growing

**Jesus grew in wisdom and stature, and in favor with God and man.**

LUKE 2:52 NIV

Pause for a moment and consider the concept that the perfect Lord and Savior of the universe ever had room to grow in wisdom. After he was found at the temple as a boy, the Bible says that Jesus grew in wisdom and stature and in favor with God and people. He was sinless from birth, absolutely, but Scripture says he had room to grow, just like the rest of us.

What an incredible testimony of his human nature! How meaningful it is to understand that he lived a perfect and sinless life in our place without all knowledge, wisdom, and maturity from infancy.

Our Savior grew in wisdom and stature and in favor with God and people. In thankfulness, we are inspired to do the same. Personal growth is an example our Savior himself set when he walked on this earth, and this begins with the fear of the Lord—knowing we need a Savior from sin. Guarding our hearts from worldly influence, deepening our understanding of Scripture, repenting, and disciplining ourselves to live first and foremost for God are ways that we too can grow in wisdom and stature and in favor with God and people.

- What area of your life has room to grow?
- What steps can you take today to develop your faith, wisdom, and character?

Prayer Prompt: Ask God to convict you where needed and inspire you to grow.

# HIS MINISTRY BEGINS

*Luke chapters 3-4*

## HIS MINISTRY BEGINS

Luke chapters 3-4

*Lord Jesus, John the Baptist announced your ministry with powerful words and a clear message, and we know John's message of repentance is for us as well. Open our hearts to always hear your truth, see our sin, and remember your glorious grace. Amen.*

# John's Message

**The word of God came to John son of Zechariah in the wilderness. He went into all the country around the Jordan, preaching a baptism of repentance for the forgiveness of sins.**

LUKE 3:2-3 NIV

John had a special calling to prepare people for the promised Messiah. An ancient prophecy said John would prepare the way in the wilderness, make a straight highway in the desert, and level the rough ground to reveal the glory of the Lord (Isaiah 40:3,5). John's preaching, baptism, and ministry fulfilled Isaiah's prophecy.

But what did that prophecy really mean?

John pointed to God's law and called out sin. His preaching removed obstacles like work-righteousness so people could see their need for a Savior. He filled in the potholes and cleared a straight path of truth to hear about God's forgiveness in Christ.

John's preaching calls to you in the dry wilderness of your sin. He pushes away everything that keeps you from seeing how much you need Jesus. He sets you straight—you are a sinner.

Then John's preaching reveals the glory of God. In the Word, you see God's plan to save sinners through Jesus' perfect life and innocent death.

- How does John's call to repentance keep your love for Christ from growing cold?
- Do you think more about the message of sin or the message of forgiveness?

Prayer Prompt: Ask God to keep you humble and repentant. Thank him for Christ the Savior.

# Fruits of Repentance

❖

**"You brood of vipers! . . .**
**Produce fruit in keeping with repentance. . . .**
**Every tree that does not produce good fruit**
**will be cut down and thrown into the fire."**

LUKE 3:7-9 NIV

John was harsh with the religious leaders in Israel. They claimed to be righteous because they were Abraham's descendants. They didn't believe John's message about sin and didn't think they were like other sinners. These Jews saw no need for a Savior—they believed they would stand guiltless before God because of their bloodline and good works.

John cut them down.

His words are also true for you. No one will stand righteous before God apart from faith in Christ. There is no room for comparison, extra efforts, or excuses.

But don't let John's threats cause you to worry about producing enough fruit. Don't misunderstand his condemnation. He was talking to self-righteous hypocrites who pridefully trusted their own fruit. John condemned those who looked to their good works for salvation, and his words stand as a warning even today.

As you live under grace, you can be confident that God is at work within you. His Spirit creates and nurtures faith—and its fruits—in you for his glory.

- How does John's message help when you know you can't be good enough?
- How does God strengthen your faith and produce fruits?

Prayer Prompt: Ask God to help you live with fruits of repentance.

# The Worthy One

❖

**"One who is more powerful than I will come, the straps of whose sandals I am not worthy to untie."**

LUKE 3:16 NIV

John the Baptist was a faithful servant of God. He accomplished the task God prepared for him as the forerunner of Christ and set a marvelous example for us.

John's genuine humility and unyielding respect for Christ are commendable. John longed for others to follow Christ: "He must become greater; I must become less" (John 3:30). He didn't promote himself or his own ministry. Scripture records how John faithfully pointed to God's message of sin and grace: "Look, the Lamb of God" (John 1:29).

We can follow John's example of humility and respect for Christ. We reflect the ardor of his ministry as we share the love and forgiveness of Jesus. Like John, we are not worthy to untie Jesus' sandals. And like John, we have a calling to proclaim the truth about Jesus. We can tell others what Jesus has done to pay for sin and reconcile us to God.

Humility before Christ keeps our attitude in check and holds our focus on his grace. His majesty, faithfulness, and mercy compel us to tell others about the one who is worthy.

- What thoughts or attitudes do you have that need a little humility?
- Reflect on the greatness of your God.

Prayer Prompt: Praise God for his worthiness. Ask God to keep you humble and to strengthen your desire to share his grace with others.

# The Baptism of Jesus

❖

**When all the people were being baptized, Jesus was baptized too.**

LUKE 3:21 NIV

John's preaching in the wilderness drew people to repent and be baptized for the forgiveness of sins. But Jesus had no sin. He went to be baptized for a different reason. Even John asked Jesus why he came to be baptized, and Jesus answered clearly: "To fulfill all righteousness" (Matthew 3:15).

The sinless Son of God asked to be baptized.

What a humbling truth for each of us to remember. What a beautiful image for us to think about as we treasure our own baptism.

As Jesus came to be baptized, he took his place alongside sinful people for whom Baptism was instituted.

Jesus' perfect life and innocent death would accomplish our salvation. By connecting himself to Baptism, Jesus gave the sacrament power to convey the forgiveness of sins, life, and salvation. The miracle of Baptism continues to freely offer those gifts today in the same way—through water and the Word.

Jesus also received blessings when he was baptized. God the Father and the Holy Spirit strengthened Jesus for the temptations he would soon face in the wilderness—and for the ministry that would cost him his life.

- What truths about the power of Baptism can strengthen you when you struggle against temptation?
- What might happen when you prayerfully reflect on the gifts of Baptism during times of discouragement?

Prayer Prompt: Ask God to help you cherish your baptism and treasure God's teachings about its blessings.

# The Triune God

**As [Jesus] was praying, heaven was opened and the Holy Spirit descended on him in bodily form like a dove. And a voice came from heaven: "You are my Son, whom I love; with you I am well pleased."**

LUKE 3:21-22 NIV

Scripture teaches that our Lord is a triune God. This is a central truth of Christianity.

During Jesus' baptism, the Holy Spirit appears in physical form as a dove. The Spirit, clearly identified and separate from Jesus, makes himself known. The voice of the Father acknowledges Jesus as his beloved Son. At Jesus' baptism, each person of the Trinity is identified apart from one another, yet they are one God.

You confess the triune God every time you say the Apostles' Creed. You hear a reminder at every baptism that our God is triune. You receive the ancient blessing from your three-in-one God.

The very heart of the matter is that God reveals himself in Scripture. This teaching is essential to Christianity because we believe what God says about himself, about sin, and about his grace for sinners. People don't get to define or explain God. Only God can teach us spiritual truths, and he gives us the faith to believe what he says in his Word.

- What is the specific role of Jesus and why is it important?
- What parts of worship remind you of the Trinity?

Prayer Prompt: Praise God for revealing himself in his Word.

# Tempted for a Purpose

❖

**Jesus, full of the Holy Spirit, returned from the Jordan and was led by the Spirit in the wilderness, where he was tempted by the Devil for forty days.**

LUKE 4:1-2 EHV

Did you read that right? Did the Holy Spirit lead Jesus into the wilderness, alone, without food, to be tempted for 40 days? Yes.

Why would the Holy Spirit want Jesus to be hungry and tempted? For us. Everything was for us. Adam and Eve were tempted and failed to obey God's law. The Israelites were tempted in the wilderness and failed to obey God's law. You are tempted and fail to obey God's law. So the Spirit led Jesus into the wilderness to do what we could not do on our own. Jesus overcame the temptations of the devil and obeyed God's commands perfectly. Jesus was not really alone, though. He was filled with the Holy Spirit.

We also have the Holy Spirit to help us overcome temptation and give us forgiveness through Jesus when we fail. We might think that Jesus cannot understand our temptations. Surely, it was easy for him to resist the devil, wasn't it? But Jesus "has been tempted in every way, just as we are, yet was without sin" (Hebrews 4:15).

- When have you had the opportunity to obey God in the midst of temptations?
- What does it mean to be full of the Holy Spirit?

Prayer Prompt: Praise Jesus for overcoming the devil in your place.

# Bread for the Soul

❖

**The Devil said to him, "If you are the Son of God, tell this stone to become bread." Jesus answered him, "It is written: 'Man shall not live by bread alone, but by every word of God.'"**

LUKE 4:3-4 EHV

The temptation the devil presented to Jesus goes deeper than we may see. Jesus was hungry, but the devil didn't offer Jesus food. Instead, he tempted Jesus to use his almighty power to feed himself. He taunted Jesus: "Are you really the Son of God?" Satan knew Jesus was true God and true man and that Jesus had put aside the use of his divine power to be our substitute. Turning the stone into bread would have been an act of rebellion against God.

Jesus' response also goes deeper than we may see. First, Jesus used the words of Scripture: "Man does not live by bread alone, but man lives by every word that comes from the mouth of the LORD" (Deuteronomy 8:3). Jesus reminded Satan that spiritual bread is more important than physical bread. Second, Jesus relied on his Father to provide the sustenance he needed.

Jesus reminds us to focus on the spiritual bread of the Word.

- Why is it important to see that Jesus was willing to put aside his divine power?
- How can you use Scripture to overcome temptation?

Prayer Prompt: Thank God for providing for your needs. Ask him to help you use his Word to fight temptation.

# The Temptation of Power

**The Devil told him, "I will give you all this power and the glory of these kingdoms, because it has been entrusted to me, and I can give it to anyone I want. So, if you worship me, it will all be yours."**

LUKE 4:6-7 EHV

Having failed to get Jesus to take up his godly power, Satan decided to tempt him with earthly power. If Jesus was planning to live a human life, he might as well live one of fame and fortune. Jesus knew his life on earth would be full of hardship and that he would eventually die the most painful and humiliating death. Wouldn't it be easier to take on the role that many people mistakenly thought the promised Messiah would play, that of an earthly king? He only needed to worship the devil.

Again, Jesus responded with words of Scripture: "Worship the Lord your God and serve him only" (Luke 4:8). Do you remember learning the First Commandment? "You shall have no other gods" (Exodus 20:3). Maybe you have taught it to your children or students in Sunday school. Fame and fortune can be temptations in our world, but it is such a comfort that we can use the Bible to overcome Satan's temptations!

- What does it look like to put the devil and his lies ahead of worshiping God?
- Why is it a good idea to memorize Scripture?

Prayer Prompt: Ask God to help you stand up against temptation.

# Testing God

❖

**"You shall not test the Lord your God."**

LUKE 4:12 EHV

The devil is smart. Twice Jesus had used Scripture against him. So on the third attempt, the devil tried the same strategy. He pulled out the Word of God to misuse it. He quoted Psalm 91, a beautiful psalm of assurance that God commands his angels to protect his people. Satan wanted Jesus to jump from a high place, knowing that the Father would protect him from death; he would not even "strike [his] foot against a stone" (Psalm 91:12). In essence, the devil was saying, "Prove to me and to yourself that you are the Son of God. Go ahead and show off." Jesus refused. He didn't try to explain. He merely clarified Scripture with more Scripture, using the command from Deuteronomy 6:16: "Do not put the LORD your God to the test."

How often are we tempted to test God? We may even have good intentions. "Surely," our sinful natures say, "it is good to give God an opportunity to show his power." But are we just trying to show off and test God? When that temptation arises, we remember that Jesus did not test his Father and neither should we.

- Have you or people you know tested God?
- Where have you seen Scripture misused to tempt God's people to sin?

Prayer Prompt: Repent of the times you have tested God's love for you. Thank Jesus for his obedience in your place.

# The Devil Doesn't Give Up

❖

**When the Devil had finished every temptation, he left him until an opportune time.**

LUKE 4:13 EHV

Jesus overcame every temptation the devil threw at him. How? He was filled with the Holy Spirit, and he properly used the words of Scripture. Having been defeated, Satan finally went away, but he did not give up. He never does! He showed up again at opportune times to test Jesus. His voice resounded in the words of the people around Jesus: "Prophesy to us, Christ! Who hit you?" and again, "Save yourself! If you are the Son of God, come down from the cross!" (Matthew 26:68; 27:40). Again, Jesus would resist, and again, Satan would lose. Yet the devil continues to look for opportune times to tempt us, hoping to succeed with us where he could not with Jesus.

At the end of 40 days of hunger, isolation, and strong temptations, Jesus was triumphant. Angels came to minister to him, and he emerged to begin his earthly ministry continually strengthened by the Holy Spirit. He did it all for us—to defeat sin, death, and the devil. We too will triumph over Satan, though he doesn't give up.

- What opportune times in your life might the devil choose to tempt you?
- What role does the Holy Spirit play in keeping you strong to fight temptation?

Prayer Prompt: Ask God to protect you from temptation. Thank the Holy Spirit for giving you strength to overcome temptation.

# THE EARLY YEARS

## *Luke chapters 4-5*

# THE EARLY YEARS

Luke chapters 4-5

*Gracious Lord, you are the Savior who loves his people. It is a joy to see you change lives through your grace and your Word. Thank you for changing us too with your message of truth. We are yours because you reached out in love to save us. Amen.*

# Do You Know What You're Doing?

❖

**"He has anointed me to . . ."**

LUKE 4:18 NIV

Often, I walk into a room only to stand there like an idiot because I can't remember what I'm supposed to do. Usually, I have to walk back to where I came from to jog my memory before I can continue.

God's people had done the same thing. They'd forgotten what Jesus came to do and what it was going to look like. So Jesus read from Isaiah to remind them what the prophet had foretold. As the Lord's Anointed, he would dispense grace and mercy through words and actions. The impact on those around him would be profound.

Like forgetting why we've walked into a room, it's easy to dive into our work for Jesus and forget why we're doing it or what it should look like. We sometimes make the task more important than the one it blesses or the goal of our work a marked achievement instead of a changed life for the recipient.

If that's you, go back to the words of Jesus to be reminded of what it's all about. First, hear the tender words of forgiveness and grace, and, second, let those words motivate your next steps for others.

- When have you experienced grace, and how did it affect you?
- How can you give that grace to someone else?

Prayer Prompt: Confess the times when you've not been grace-filled. Ask for opportunities to bring the good news to others.

# It Is Fulfilled

❖

**"Today this scripture is fulfilled."**

LUKE 4:21 NIV

After explaining exactly who the Messiah was and what he came to do, Jesus addressed those gathered to hear his first sermon in Nazareth. Unfortunately, those listening were offended. They couldn't understand how the boy they watched grow up could fulfill the Scriptures, much less be their Messiah.

Three years later, Jesus made a similar statement with his last words: "It is finished!" People didn't like that either. They mocked the foolishness of a king who claimed to be God but couldn't save himself.

How do I react to the work Jesus does in my life or the lives of others? I have to confess that sometimes I don't understand or like it. I am often judgmental or proud about the way I think things should be done instead of seeing how Jesus is working on my behalf.

That's why today's words are so important. They remind me that my sinful thoughts don't change what Jesus did. He fulfilled Scripture and then announced on the cross that his work of salvation was finished. Jesus doesn't care if this offends my pride or confuses my selfish ideas about who he is. He came so that I would know without a doubt that everything Scripture has to say is fulfilled in him!

- How are you judgmental or proud regarding God's work in your life?
- How does Jesus' fulfillment of Scripture change those attitudes?

Prayer Prompt: Thank God for fulfilling all Scripture for you.

# Providence for the Pagan, Healing for the Heathen

❖

**"There were many widows in Israel in the days of Elijah. . . . And there were many lepers in Israel in the time of Elisha."**

LUKE 4:25,27 EHV

Human reason cannot comprehend God's grace. The people in the synagogue in Nazareth tried to use human logic to understand who the Messiah was. Jesus read from the prophet Isaiah, and the people were amazed, at first. Yet they quickly rejected him: "Isn't this Joseph's son?" (Luke 4:22). Certainly, the Messiah needed more noble roots than a carpenter from Nazareth!

In response, Jesus pointed out that in the time of Elisha and Elijah, God's grace was given to foreigners instead of to the Israelites. Grace wasn't given because of merit or lineage, and it wasn't only for the Jews. Grace doesn't follow the path of reason or fit into the confines of logic. God extends it to the world.

Providence to a pagan widow in Zarephath. Healing to a heathen general in Syria.

Boundless, limitless grace is given at God's discretion to those who are undeserving, like us—sinful beyond measure and recipients of grace that is beyond human comprehension.

- Why can it be hard to accept that all who believe in God are his children?
- Who do you know that needs to hear about God's boundless, limitless grace?

Prayer Prompt: Thank God for his grace, given not because of what you have done but in spite of it.

# I Must

❖

**"I must proclaim the good news of the kingdom of God to the other towns also, because that is why I was sent."**
LUKE 4:43 NIV

Luke records several "I must" statements by Jesus—and your salvation is secure because Jesus did them all perfectly. He obeyed the law, cherished Scripture, and loved people. He went where he was called, even when it meant crucifixion. He was raised to life.

"I must be taking care of my Father's business" (Luke 2:49 EHV).

"The Son of Man must suffer many things and . . . be killed and . . . raised to life" (Luke 9:22 NIV).

"I must press on today and tomorrow and the next day" (Luke 13:33 NIV).

"Zacchaeus, . . . I must stay at your house today" (Luke 19:5 NIV).

"The Son of Man must be . . . crucified and . . . raised again" (Luke 24:7 NIV).

"Everything must be fulfilled that is written about me" (Luke 24:44 NIV).

Grace compels us to respond to Jesus' redemptive work with worship and thankful living. At times, you might feel that you *must* do something. But you don't! Jesus already did all the musts perfectly on your behalf. Your salvation is secure because of Jesus' perfect obedience, sacrificial death, and glorious resurrection!

- Who can you talk to when you're burdened by musts?
- How do you show your thankfulness to God?

Prayer Prompt: Ask God to help you remember all the things Jesus did for you.

# Perfect Priorities

**Jesus . . . sat down and began teaching the crowds from the boat. When he had finished speaking, he said to Simon, "Put out into the deep water, and let down your nets for a catch."**

LUKE 5:3-4 EHV

Jesus was about to miraculously fill Peter's boat with fish and call him to a life of ministry. Yet he first took the time to teach the crowds that had gathered. Jesus didn't rush past the people who were listening to him because he loved them as much as he loved Peter.

Jesus' priorities were perfect. He was always focused on saving souls.

Do you ever rush past people because you're thinking about the next thing? Ever give a terse answer because you're busy? Ever thoughtlessly brush past the least of God's people because something else seems significant? Ever fail to love someone who needs you?

Jesus forgives you every time you fail to love others or tell them about God's love in Christ.

You are called to love the people in front of you. Whether little children, elderly parents, neighbors, or coworkers, Jesus puts people who need his love on your path. Share his forgiveness and grace with others. Don't rush past people—Jesus loves them as much as he loves you.

- Have you ever felt that someone has looked past you?
- Whom might you look past?

Prayer Prompt: Ask God to help you see the people in front of you and love them like Jesus.

# Seeing Our Sin

❖

**When Simon Peter saw this, he fell at Jesus' knees and said, "Go away from me, Lord; I am a sinful man!"**

LUKE 5:8 NIV

Jesus told Peter to drop his nets into the water after a long night without any fish, and Peter obeyed. Peter and his friends had caught so many fish they needed a second boat to empty their nets. Jesus displayed his miraculous power as the Son of God, and several of those fishermen left everything to be his disciples.

But look at Peter's initial response: "Go away from me, Lord; I am a sinful man!"

You may have felt that way.

Though some people turn in cold unbelief, Jesus' holiness strikes fear, guilt, and shame into the hearts of many. When people see Jesus through eyes of faith and with repentant hearts, they see their perfect, merciful Savior. Cherish your privilege as a believer to fall at your Savior's feet and confess your sins. Don't let unworthiness pull you away from the Lord in shame. Trust God's loving grace that invites and allows you to come and receive mercy. It is a blessing to see the holiness of Christ and to fall to your knees in need of his forgiveness. What an honor it is to hear his forgiveness and holy calling!

- Does guilt ever prevent you from coming to Jesus for forgiveness?
- When or where do you most often hear reminders of Jesus' holiness?

Prayer Prompt: Thank Jesus for calling you to repentance and faith.

# Simple and Powerful Prayer

❖

**"Lord, if you are willing, you can make me clean."**

LUKE 5:12 NIV

Prayers do not need to be long or eloquent to be effective. The sick man in this reading shows us how to pray in ten words or less.

The man addresses Jesus and then prays, "If you are willing." His words teach us to yield to God's will. God's knowledge of our situation is greater than our knowledge, and his plans are better than our plans (Isaiah 55:9). So when we ask for his will to be done, we humble ourselves and acknowledge his sovereign power over all things.

Next, the sick man says, "You can make me clean." He shows complete confidence in Jesus' ability to heal him. When we pray, we can do the same. We can take our requests to Jesus knowing that he has power over all things big and small—in nature, in our relationships, and even in the things we hide deep down in our hearts. Jesus can change even the most hopeless situations. So pray with confidence!

- Is there anything in your life for which you need to pray boldly?
- What can you do today to remind yourself of God's power over all things, including the situations in your life?

Prayer Prompt: Praise the Lord for his sovereignty over all things, his grace given to you in Christ, and his willingness to listen to you. Ask for whatever you need. Trust him to answer according to his will.

# Best Friends Forever

❖

**Some men came carrying a paralyzed man . . . to lay him before Jesus. When they could not find a way to do this because of the crowd, they went up on the roof and lowered him . . . right in front of Jesus.**

LUKE 5:18-19 NIV

BFFs—best friends forever. We'll do anything for them, and this story is a perfect example. Jesus was healing people all over the countryside, and large crowds were following him. These men knew Jesus could heal their friend. They simply had to get him to Jesus. Not an easy task. Shimmying through the crowd wasn't an option, so they needed to shake things up. They climbed to the top of the house, removed part of the roof, and lowered their friend on a mat to get to Jesus.

Friendship is expressed in many ways, and this story shows how some friends shared Jesus with someone in need. Jesus healed the paralyzed man and forgave his sins—how thankful the man must have been to Jesus *and* his friends! Friends who share their faith in Jesus are quite literally best friends forever. They share blessings in this life and for eternity.

- Is there anything standing in your way of leading a friend in need to Jesus?
- What striking thing could you do for a friend that would bring her closer to Jesus?

Prayer Prompt: Thank Jesus for the blessing of friends. Ask him to open doors for your friends in need to meet Jesus.

# He's the Real Deal

❖

**"Which is easier: to say, 'Your sins are forgiven,' or to say, 'Get up and walk'? But I want you to know that the Son of Man has authority . . . to forgive sins."**

LUKE 5:23-24 NIV

Jesus' healings caused quite a stir. It must have been amazing to see a disabled man roll up his mat and walk on two sturdy legs. More remarkable, Jesus included the forgiveness of sins in the package. The Jewish people were used to doing things to receive forgiveness: prayers, sacrifices, or offerings. Jesus offered a new deal. He would be the sacrifice for sin so we could access forgiveness through faith.

This was revolutionary thinking for a people steeped in tradition. That's why Jesus performed miracles. He was human and also God with authority to forgive sins. His miracles helped people see that he was the real deal with a new deal.

Sometimes we too have trouble believing that forgiveness is free. We want to bargain with God, offer him something to gain favor, or stand on our own two feet. But spiritual sturdiness is a gift from God. Jesus wants us to know that forgiveness is free.

- What things tempt you to bargain with God rather than trust his forgiveness?
- When your faith in Jesus wobbles, what comfort can you gain from recalling his miracles?

Prayer Prompt: Praise Jesus for his authority over all things physical and spiritual. Ask for sturdiness when your faith wobbles.

# *He Sees You*

❖

**Jesus went out and saw a tax collector by the name of Levi sitting at his tax booth. "Follow me," Jesus said to him, and Levi got up, left everything and followed him.**

LUKE 5:27-28 NIV

Levi is the Hebrew name for Matthew, who became one of Jesus' disciples after the calling described here. What compelled Levi to leave everything and follow Jesus? Maybe he was tired of being so hated because he collected taxes. Maybe he had all the material wealth he needed yet felt empty inside. Felt guilty. Lacked purpose. There might be a yearning like this in your heart too.

An important detail in this text is that Jesus saw Levi. Despite all the people and activity around them, he spoke directly to Levi. Jesus sees you too. He calls you. That little nudge in your heart to pick up your Bible today—that's Jesus lovingly calling you to his Word, where he speaks directly to you. He wants you to experience how everything changes with his grace. You can leave behind your guilt, your ever-present work, and your important activities to follow where he leads you today.

- What things make you feel lonely, insignificant, or unworthy of being seen by Jesus?
- What activities can you put aside this week so you can spend some restorative time with Jesus?

Prayer Prompt: Thank Jesus for calling you, for moving you to spend time with him. Ask him to help you follow him with trust like Levi.

# Help to Heal

❖

**"It is not the healthy who need a doctor, but the sick. I have not come to call the righteous, but sinners to repentance."**

LUKE 5:31-32 NIV

When we feel a cold coming on, we have the tendency to fight hard against it. We don't want to admit that we might be getting sick. When we're sick, we can't do the things we want to do.

Likewise, during Jesus' ministry, the people did not want to admit their own sin. They wanted to do their own thing. Jesus could not help those people because they insisted they were fine. To explain this problem, Jesus compares himself to a doctor whose primary mission is to heal sick people.

Sin is spiritual illness. No matter how hard we fight against it, we cannot overcome it on our own. When we admit that we are sick with sin, we are, in essence, saying, "I need help." That's repentance, and it starts the healing process. When you spend time with Jesus in his Word (just like you are doing now), he will work repentance in your heart. The stubbornness melts away. Then you are ready for the medicine he offers—his full and free forgiveness.

- Why is repentance so vital in your battle against sin?
- How do regular appointments with Jesus improve your spiritual health?

Prayer Prompt: Confess your stubbornness about your sin. Ask Jesus to restore your health each time you come to him in repentance.

# Full Forgiveness and Fellowship

❖

**[John's disciples] said to him,
"John's disciples often fast and pray, and so do the disciples of the Pharisees, but yours go on eating and drinking."
Jesus answered, "Can you make the friends of the bridegroom fast while he is with them?"**

LUKE 5:33-34 NIV

The people following Jesus noticed lots of differences among various religious groups. They wondered why only some believers fasted if they all believed in the same God. Their question and Jesus' patient answer affirm our wonderings about religious practices. It's healthy to examine our behavior. Questions open an opportunity to learn from Scripture and be strengthened in faith.

In this case, Jesus compares himself to a groom and his followers to the wedding party. He knows religious practices such as fasting can have a purpose; fasting and prayer may help us focus on a spiritual thought or build good habits. The crowd saw fasting as a display of devotion, a signal of righteousness. Jesus wanted the people to know that with his grace there is no need for superficial displays of righteousness. He offers full forgiveness from sin and free fellowship. Friends of Jesus are invited to simply enjoy his presence.

- What religious traditions do you question, and where can you take those questions?
- Do the religious practices in your life distract you or point you toward the full forgiveness you have in Jesus?

Prayer Prompt: Praise Jesus for inviting you into fellowship with him. Ask for wisdom from Scripture when you have questions.

# JESUS GAINS POPULARITY

*Luke chapters 6-8*

# JESUS GAINS POPULARITY

Luke chapters 6-8

*Lord Jesus, some people followed you and listened to your teaching, but they didn't really know you or understand your message. Help us know you better as our Lord and Savior. Deepen our love for your Word and enrich our understanding of your truth. Amen.*

# Hungry for More

**"Blessed are you who hunger now, for you will be satisfied. Blessed are you who weep now, for you will laugh."**

LUKE 6:21 NIV

Maintaining a healthy weight has always been a struggle for me. So if you're anything like me, you know the problem isn't *what* you eat. It's *why* you eat. I eat for a bazillion reasons that have nothing to do with physical hunger.

I hunger for peace, comfort, answers, joy, wisdom, rest, a reprieve from boredom, and the list goes on. Food doesn't do a good job of filling these voids.

In the same way, Jesus' answer to the sick and hurting didn't just address their physical needs. When he healed people, he offered them forgiveness too. He knew what they were truly hungry for—he fills spiritual hunger.

Someday in heaven we won't hunger or weep, but it's hard to live with those hunger pangs now. To keep my mind focused on the only perfect source of satisfaction and joy, I hang little sticky note "snacks" of Scripture around my house.

God sees my hunger and my pain.

I will put down the cheese puff, breathe, and trust that God is with me in this—and every—struggle.

- What are you truly hungry for?
- What are you tempted to fill that hunger with instead of God's comfort?

Prayer Prompt: Ask God to search your heart to know the true cause of your hunger. Ask him to help you fill it with his daily bread.

# Be a Messy Chef

**"Give, and it will be given to you.
A good measure, pressed down, shaken together
and running over, will be poured into your lap.
For with the measure you use, it will be measured to you."**
LUKE 6:38 NIV

I never took the time in my younger years to learn how to cook or bake. As a result, I'm still learning how to do very basic things now in my 40s.

Because I'm still in the phase of my chef-ing adventures, where I follow a recipe as closely as if it were a law, words like those found in Luke 6:38 stress me out a ton. Luke clearly bakes like my four-year-old. In my mind, a good measure is, well, . . . good. Let's not get crazy with the "pressed down" and "shaken together." "Running over" and "poured into your lap" create horrific visions of mops and stains and very bad dinner reviews.

But Luke tells us to imitate God's generosity of forgiveness in Christ like a messy four-year-old chef. And we can—even on the worst days—because God, our messy chef, fills our pantry abundantly.

- Where might God be asking you to engage your time, talents, and resources as a messy chef?
- How can you remind yourself today that God will always generously fill your pantry?

Prayer Prompt: Ask God to remove any fear or hesitation that may be in the way of trusting his pressed down, shaken together, and running over love for you.

# Spiritual Marinade

**"A good man brings good things out of the good stored up in his heart, and an evil man brings evil things out of the evil stored up in his heart. For the mouth speaks what the heart is full of."**

LUKE 6:45 NIV

Every so often when you add a certain combination of ingredients to a recipe, the outcome and flavors might surprise you. Most of the time, though, what you put into a recipe is a pretty good predictor of the flavors that will come out.

These words of Jesus reveal a similar message. What you store up internally marinates and flavors everything that comes out of you. When you store up resentment, frustration, jealousy, or greed, those flavors will appear in your actions, behaviors, and choices. When you store up the love, forgiveness, grace, and righteousness that are yours through Christ Jesus, those ingredients will flavor the way you live your life.

Take an inventory of what is stored up in your heart right now. Are you ruminating or worrying about things out of your control or frustrations and sufferings you have experienced? Or are you dwelling richly in the love and blessings of your heavenly Father?

- How would you describe the internal store of your heart?
- How can you be intentional about internalizing and dwelling in the love and blessings of Jesus?

Prayer Prompt: Ask God to help you store grace and love in your heart. Confess the thinking that sours your soul.

# Gatekeeping God's Love

**There a centurion's servant, whom his master valued highly, was sick and about to die. The centurion heard of Jesus and sent some elders of the Jews to him, asking him to come and heal his servant. When they came to Jesus, they pleaded earnestly with him, "This man deserves to have you do this, because he loves our nation and has built our synagogue."**

LUKE 7:2-5 NIV

The Jews generally viewed the Romans as oppressors, so the elders probably assumed Jesus would deny the centurion's request. They wanted Jesus to know he had their approval to do a miracle. Why? The centurion loved God and did great things for the Jews.

God's people know, and often say, that God loves everyone. Yet good intentions can veil our selfish arrogance and blind us to times when we gatekeep God's gracious love. We think, "She is kind to everyone, so of course I will cook her family a meal after a tragedy," or "Why would I include my child's unkind teacher in my prayers?"—as if we decide who God loves!

God sent his Son to die for all people, and no gatekeeping can impede his love. God proved his unbounded love when Christ died for all sinners.

- If God loves someone, why does it matter if you do?
- How can you combat your desire to gatekeep God's love?

Prayer Prompt: Thank God for loving others through you. Confess your flawed judgments that get in the way.

# Amazing Faith

**The centurion sent friends to say to him:
"Lord, don't trouble yourself, for I do not deserve
to have you come under my roof. . . .
But say the word, and my servant will be healed."
When Jesus heard this, he was amazed at him, and . . . said,
"I tell you, I have not found such great faith even in Israel."**

LUKE 7:6-7,9 NIV

Based on Michelin stars, Joël Robuchon was the best chef in the world. I am the best chef in my house, but even my best dish is not worthy to serve to someone like him.

The centurion felt the same way about Jesus. The Jewish elders thought the centurion deserved Jesus' love and attention because he did good things for them. But the centurion knew that wasn't true. He knew that his sin made him unholy before Jesus, the holy Son of God. The centurion was unworthy to meet Jesus or for Jesus to come to him. Yet the centurion's faith trusted Jesus' authority to heal both his servant and his sin from afar. Amazed by this humble confession of faith, Jesus did what the centurion asked.

- How does your perception of your value to God compare with the centurion's?
- What are the characteristics of a heart that rests in God's unconditional love?

Prayer Prompt: Confess when you have relied on yourself to earn God's love and attention. Ask him to remind you that Jesus makes you worthy.

# An Important Question

**"John the Baptist sent us . . . to ask, 'Are you the one who is to come, or should we expect someone else?'" At that very time Jesus cured many who had diseases, sicknesses and evil spirits and gave sight to many who were blind. So he replied to the messengers, "Go back and report to John what you have seen and heard."**

LUKE 7:20-22 NIV

Before the birth of John the Baptist, an angel told John's parents that he would prepare the way for the Messiah. John knew the prophecies, his purpose, and for whom he was preparing the world. Jesus acclaims John in Luke 7:28: "There is no one greater than John." We may think that of all people, John the Baptist should've been very clear on Jesus' identity as the Son of God and Savior from sin. Some might say that since we have Bibles to read, we shouldn't doubt Jesus' identity and work of salvation either. Yet Jesus addressed John's—and our—uncertainty clearly and with evidence. He didn't scold John or accuse him of unbelief. Jesus provided exactly what John needed to ground his faith in God and fulfill his God-given purpose. Jesus does the same for us in his Word and sacraments.

- What questions does God answer for you in these verses?
- What opportunities do you have to report "what you have seen and heard"?

Prayer Prompt: Thank God for a life with unlimited access to his Word and sacraments.

# Wisdom's Children

**"John the Baptist came neither eating bread nor drinking wine, and you say, 'He has a demon.' The Son of Man came eating and drinking, and you say, 'Here is a glutton and a drunkard.' . . . But wisdom is proved right by all her children."**

LUKE 7:33-35 NIV

The Pharisees in Jesus' time thought they were wise. They believed that perfect compliance with God's Old Testament laws would earn them eternity in heaven. If we believe we can earn God's favor by doing more good than bad, by putting more positivity than negativity into the world, we become children of the Pharisees' wisdom. This will only leave us guilt-ridden and burdened by a righteousness we can never achieve.

Who, then, was wise? Not the Pharisees! But by the Pharisees' standards, neither John nor Jesus made the cut. The Pharisees were blind to God's true wisdom that triumphs over falsehood and shines through his believers.

Because of Jesus' perfect obedience to God's plan for salvation, you and John and I will see our faith—our wisdom—proved right when we stand perfect before God in heaven.

- What kind of wisdom will you pass on to others or to your children?
- When others call you foolish for your faith, how can these verses bring you rest?

Prayer Prompt: Thank Jesus for making you a child of his grace and wisdom. Ask him to help you let go of your belief that your salvation depends on you.

# Overwhelmed by Gratitude

**A woman in that town who lived a sinful life learned that Jesus was eating at the Pharisee's house, so she came there with an alabaster jar of perfume. As she stood behind him at his feet weeping, she began to wet his feet with her tears. Then she wiped them with her hair, kissed them and poured perfume on them. Then Jesus said to her, "Your sins are forgiven. . . . Your faith has saved you; go in peace."**

LUKE 7:37-38,48,50 NIV

Jesus and his disciples were guests at the home of a Jewish leader. This was an intimidating dinner party! And yet something induced a woman with a bad reputation to enter this private home, uninvited, and disturb the men gathered there. Something moved her to weep so deeply that she could wash Jesus' feet with only her tears. Something told her that Jesus was more valuable than a jar of perfume worth a year's pay.

Our sister in faith understood something true: God demands perfection and condemns sin. She understood her own desperate need for a Savior, and by faith, she knew the Savior was Jesus. Her actions were an outpouring of gratitude and a reflection of God's love that sweeps away embarrassment, fear, and shame.

- How does Jesus remove your shame and fill you with gratitude?
- How does your faith compel you to express that gratitude in your life?

Prayer Prompt: Ask Jesus for the courage to rely on his grace to meet every challenge.

# Just Scatter

**"A farmer went out to sow his seed. As he was scattering the seed . . ."**

LUKE 8:5 NIV

Do you ever feel scared to tell people about your faith? I do. My biggest fear is that I'll unintentionally introduce people to God in a way that makes them more confused or resistant.

In Luke chapter 8, Jesus tells the parable of a farmer who is sowing his seeds. He is also teaching us how different people respond to God's message of forgiveness through faith in Christ. Spoiler alert: Not every seed results in faith. Even though the seeds were perfectly scattered by the one and only Son of God, very few of them actually grow a successful crop.

But Jesus scattered anyway. He scattered the seed, the eternity-changing gospel message, freely giving forgiveness everywhere with his authentic love, truth, and grace.

I can do that too. The act of scattering is so full of permission and abundance that it might even be considered wasteful. But that's the beauty of it. We don't need to be nervous about scattering the wrong way. We can throw around the love and freedom of the gospel as generously as a preschool kiddo left alone with a whole container of glitter.

Don't stress about sharing. Just scatter.

- What could scattering look like in your life?
- What fears are holding you back from scattering your faith?

Prayer Prompt: Confess your fears to God about sharing the gospel. Ask him to replace those fears with a bold and loving spirit of generous gospel scattering.

# A Farmer's Guide to Soul Care

**"The seed on good soil stands for those with a noble and good heart, who hear the word, retain it, and by persevering produce a crop."**

LUKE 8:15 NIV

Have you ever considered how the explanation of this parable about a farmer can help us better understand how to thrive as Christians? Our perfect farmer shares the key components of a healthy soul: a heart that is noble and good, a desire to hear the Word and hold on to it, and a legacy that is rich with the fruits of faith.

Those sound really great, right?

Most of us would quickly and easily admit that we'd love to be described by the words in this verse. But how do we get there and stay there? How do we flourish in faith, rooted in Christ's grace and forgiveness? What's our perfect farmer's guide to soul care?

We learn a lot by looking at Scripture's descriptions of unhealthy soil. We learn that the devil is always ready and waiting to attack and tempt us to sin. We learn the importance of having deep, strong roots to our faith, and we are cautioned about worries and storing up treasure on earth rather than in heaven.

- What types of unhealthy soils do you struggle with?
- How can you grow in your desire to hear the Word and hold on to it today?

Prayer Prompt: Thank God that faith is a *gift* not of our own doing.

# On a Stand

**"No one lights a lamp and hides it in a clay jar or puts it under a bed. Instead, they put it on a stand. Then those who come in can see its light."**

LUKE 8:16 NIRV

Do you know what's great about this verse? It's simple and straightforward. I can't imagine very many people getting confused when they read it, regardless of the fact that our world and lighting technology have changed. You get it: if you have a light in your hand and you're in a dark room, the last thing you would do is block out that light.

When we think about the dark places where God might be calling us to shine our faith in Christ our Savior, it often stirs up feelings of fear, confusion, guilt, and inadequacy. I felt all those things too until I realized that we don't need to do anything special. We can just "put it on a stand." We can talk often and joyfully about the forgiveness Jesus has given us. We can love the way he taught us to—free from grudges and full of grace. We can shine his truths treasured up in our hearts. Then those who come into our lives can see his light.

- What is one way you can shine Jesus' salvation brightly today?
- Who in your close family or friendship circles encourages you to keep your light shining brightly?

Prayer Prompt: Ask God to bring the lost into your life.

# We Are Family

❖

**"My mother and brothers are those who hear God's word and do what it says."**

LUKE 8:21 NIRV

Have you ever had the opportunity to meet someone influential or famous? If you have, chances are that you paid extra for a special meet and greet at a concert or booked a tour that included a brief question and answer session.

Can you imagine if, during your meeting, the person you had booked time with was suddenly notified that his or her family had spontaneously arrived and was hoping for some one-on-one time? Wouldn't you expect your VIP meeting to wrap up pretty quickly at that point? I mean, it's family.

But what if, instead, the important person stayed? What if he or she stuck with you instead of bailing once someone more worthy than you came along? How would that make you feel?

Jesus stayed. And it wasn't because he didn't love his family. He stayed because his definition of *family* extends far beyond genetics. His definition of *family* is "those who hear God's word and do what it says." That's you and me—brought into the family by the sacrifice of Christ.

- How does Jesus' definition of *family* impact your definition?
- Do you know anyone who feels lost and may need to hear that they are a VIP to *God?*

Prayer Prompt: Thank God for sending his Son who—before we were even alive—was willing to die so we could be a part of his family.

# JESUS FACES OPPOSITION

*Luke chapters 9-11*

# JESUS FACES OPPOSITION

Luke chapters 9-11

*Lord God, your Word draws people to repentance and covers them with grace. At the same time, some people reject your teaching and stand in opposition to your truth. Help us follow and trust you even when those around us resist you. Amen.*

# Feeding of the Five Thousand

**They all ate and were satisfied, and the disciples picked up twelve basketfuls of broken pieces that were left over.**

LUKE 9:17 NIV

Jesus had withdrawn to an isolated place with his 12 disciples, but the crowds still followed him. He welcomed them, but he knew their hearts. They were seeking miracles and material benefits rather than the Messiah from sin they really needed.

The crowd was massive: five thousand men, plus women and children. The disciples were worried about how to feed and lodge the people. Sadly, despite their witness of Jesus' past miracles, none of the disciples suggested he could be the solution to this dilemma.

Apart from the benefit to the crowds, the miracle that followed was meant to strengthen the disciples. The disciples were close enough to witness Jesus' prayer of thanks, his look to heaven, his breaking of the five loaves and two fish, and the seemingly endless distribution that followed.

After thousands upon thousands of people had eaten their fill, the disciples gathered up the leftovers. In response to their initial worry, Jesus had provided exactly 12 baskets of leftover food. Twelve baskets. Twelve strengthened disciples.

- What baskets of blessings have you received that remind you of God's generosity and power?
- Jesus loved the people. How may he have felt knowing their hearts were seeking earthly things instead of the forgiveness he offered?

Prayer Prompt: Praise God for the ways he supplies your life with an excess of blessings.

# Who Do You Say I Am?

❖

**Once when Jesus was praying by himself, and his disciples were nearby, he asked them, "Who do the crowds say that I am?" They answered, "John the Baptist; others say Elijah; and still others that one of the prophets of long ago has risen." Then he said to them, "But who do you say that I am?" Peter answered, "The Christ of God."**

LUKE 9:18-20 NET

Jesus had entered a point in his ministry where he frequently sought solitude to pray and escape the demands of the increasing crowds. He intentionally instructed his disciples in private.

Ever the master teacher, Jesus posed a question to promote thoughtful discussion from the group. The disciples responded accordingly. Their answers about Jesus' identity represented the misconceptions and speculations of the crowds.

Jesus then asked a question that drew a stark contrast between the perceptions of the crowds and the understanding of the disciples: "Who do you say that I am?" Representing the entire group, Peter stated that Jesus was the Christ who had been sent from God. His answer unveiled a clear confession of Jesus' true nature. *Christ* means "Messiah" or "Anointed One." Peter's accurate confession reveals Jesus as the true Messiah, God's long-promised Savior from sin.

- How do many people today identify Jesus?
- How would you respond if someone asked you who Jesus is?

Prayer Prompt: Seek a quiet place to pray. Confess Jesus as the Anointed One sent to redeem you from sin.

# Give Up Your Own Way

❖

**Then [Jesus] said to the crowd, "If any of you wants to be my follower, you must give up your own way, take up your cross daily, and follow me."**

LUKE 9:23 NLT

The crowds were pressing in and looking for ways to connect with Jesus. Their minds were on an earthly Messiah, a Savior from the political oppression of Rome.

Jesus, though, was singularly focused on his final journey to Jerusalem. In fact, following Peter's confession of faith, Jesus predicted his impending death to the disciples for the very first time. Jesus' sole purpose was to fulfill God's plan of salvation. The cross he would bear would bring God's forgiveness to everyone.

Jesus turned his attention to the people in the crowd to strengthen their faith. He wanted to impress upon them that truly following him would involve giving up their own ways, denying their shortsighted ideas, and following God's will. Taking up their cross was not referring to the daily struggles of life but, rather, accepting whatever hardships come as a follower of Christ—strains in relationships or hard choices about finances or priorities. This would prove to be a difficult teaching for many.

- What does it mean to be a follower of Jesus?
- Why would it be so hard for many in the crowd to truly follow Jesus?

Prayer Prompt: Confess the things that hold you back from giving up your own way. Ask God to help you keep Jesus first in your life.

# The Glory of Jesus

❖

**As [Jesus] was praying, the appearance of his face was altered, and his clothing became dazzling white. And behold, two men were talking with him, Moses and Elijah, who appeared in glory and spoke of his departure, which he was about to accomplish at Jerusalem.**

LUKE 9:29-31 ESV

Once again, Jesus retreated from the crowds to pray. The disciples who accompanied him had seen Jesus in many situations. He was their friend, teacher, rabbi, and miracle worker. However, what they witnessed on the mountain that day was something they couldn't have imagined. The spectacular sights and sounds left the disciples awestruck.

Jesus, their friend and Lord, stood before them, discussing his final journey to the cross with Moses and Elijah, two of the Old Testament's most revered leaders. They appeared from heaven in glorious splendor, yet Jesus was even more radiant with his own glory as the Son of God.

The God from eternity had chosen to mute his majesty in favor of becoming the least of all people to save all people. For just a few moments, he allowed his closest followers to glimpse the awesome wonders of his glory at a time when being a follower of Jesus would soon become very inglorious.

- Jesus' "face was altered" as he radiated glory. How do you imagine that?
- How might you react had you been witness to this scene?

Prayer Prompt: Praise God for the glimpses of his glory provided in his Word.

# This Is My Son, My Chosen One

❖

**A voice came out of the cloud, saying, "This is my Son, my Chosen One; listen to him!"**
LUKE 9:35 ESV

As Jesus, Moses, and Elijah were discussing Jesus' imminent departure and the fulfillment of salvation, the glory cloud of the Lord descended on the small group gathered on the mountain. The disciples were terrified because they knew from the Old Testament Scriptures that no one could see the glory of the Lord and survive. Yet there they were, witnessing Jesus' glory, being enveloped in the Lord's cloud, and hearing the voice of the Father—and they lived to tell about it!

About eight days prior to this incredible event, Peter confessed his faith in Jesus as the promised Savior who would redeem sinners. On the mountain that day, Peter received confirmation of what he knew. He heard the Father's voice proclaim Jesus as his "Chosen One"—the Messiah, the Christ of God.

With authority, God the Father told the disciples to listen to Jesus as he prepared them for the days to come. Jesus would soon proclaim that their salvation was complete and teach them how to share the promises of God with others.

- What might have been a difficult teaching for the disciples when listening to Jesus?
- Have you ever known something intellectually but didn't have a true understanding of it until you experienced it firsthand?

Prayer Prompt: Pray for ears that listen to God's Word and a heart that cherishes it.

# They Didn't Understand

❖

**"Listen carefully to what I am about to tell you: The Son of Man is going to be delivered into the hands of men." But [the disciples] did not understand what this meant. It was hidden from them, so that they did not grasp it, and they were afraid to ask him about it.**

LUKE 9:44-45 NIV

Jesus told his disciples what was going to happen to him, but the disciples didn't understand. God's full plan of salvation was hidden from them, and what Jesus was saying didn't make sense. Delivered to whom? Why?

No one could have figured out that God planned to save sinners by sacrificing his only Son. Only God's Spirit makes his mysteries known.

We trust God's revealed plan—Christ's sacrifice saves us from hell. Things are still hidden from us in this life, but God's plan of salvation isn't one of them. Like the disciples, we have questions about things we don't understand. Yet we know that God's Spirit works through the Word to deepen our understanding, reveal himself to us, and strengthen our faith. With childlike faith, we trust him even when things around us don't make sense.

Jesus wants us to know that he gave up his life for us so we can dwell with him forever.

- Why doesn't Jesus always explain everything?
- How does Jesus' completed work of salvation calm your doubts and questions?

Prayer Prompt: Confess the times when your questions and doubts have overshadowed your faith.

# Anyone Not Against Us

❖

**"Master," said John, "we saw someone driving out demons in your name and we tried to stop him, because he is not one of us." "Do not stop him," Jesus said, "for whoever is not against you is for you."**

LUKE 9:49-50 NIV

Jesus is the master of reading hearts and giving perfect answers. When his disciples came to him, they were upset, and Jesus knew why. In their zeal of following him, the disciples had begun to feel a sense of privilege. After all, they were trained by Jesus, the Son of God and Savior of the world!

And now someone else was doing ministry—*even miracles*—in Jesus' name.

Jesus addressed the selfish pride in their hearts. Their concern was not for ministry but for themselves.

Jesus addresses the same sins in our hearts: superiority, jealousy, criticism, mistrust, resentment, and more.

Jesus' words offer an answer of grace: "Whoever is not against you is for you." Do not be led by the sin in your heart to judge others. Ministry in the kingdom of God is not done by the proud. Rather, it is done by humble, forgiven, and thankful followers of God.

- Do you recognize times when pride and resentment taint your thoughts about the ministry work of others?
- Will you always be able to distinguish when ministry work is being done in the name of Jesus?

Prayer Prompt: Ask God to bless ministry that is done in his name.

# Discipleship

❖

**A man said to [Jesus], "I will follow you wherever you go." Jesus replied, "Foxes have dens and birds have nests, but the Son of Man has no place to lay his head." Jesus said . . . , "Let the dead bury their own dead, but you go and proclaim the kingdom of God.". . . Jesus replied, "No one who puts a hand to the plow and looks back is fit for service in the kingdom of God."**

LUKE 9:57-58,60,62 NIV

Jesus gives stern, repeated warnings to several men who want to follow him. Torn between their earthly responsibilities and a desire to follow Jesus, they are cautioned about the cost of discipleship.

Today we also struggle with the cost of discipleship, though it looks different. It's not about resting or responsibilities. It's about hard choices. In Christian freedom, we look for wisdom in holy living. We seek God's guidance as we choose a home or a church and school to attend. We give thought to how we make money, spend it, and are entertained. Our relationships are shaped by godly priorities. We live in thankfulness as forgiven sinners who reflect our Savior's love.

When we fail as disciples, Jesus forgives us. He reminds us it will be hard, but he gives us strength to persevere in grace.

- Describe putting your family first before Christ.
- Describe honoring Christ as you fulfill earthly responsibilities.

Prayer Prompt: Ask God for strength and wisdom for the hard decisions.

# What Brings You Joy?

**Jesus, full of joy through the Holy Spirit, said, "I praise you . . . because you have hidden these things from the wise and learned, and revealed them to little children."**

LUKE 10:21 NIV

The disciples were excited! "Even the demons submit to us in your name" (Luke 10:17)! Yet Jesus redirected the disciples and encouraged them to rejoice instead that their names are written in heaven.

Like giddy children, this simple band of disciples marveled at what God had done in and through them. If they relied on the Pharisees' wisdom or learning, credit might have been kept to themselves. But the disciples knew their words and actions came from Jesus. They were dependent on God to provide the results—just like little children depend on their parents. Jesus praised God for revealing this in such a marvelous way!

In a society of achievement, it's not desirable to identify with the simple or to be considered a child. However, that's exactly how God works—through faith that is completely dependent on him.

Everything we don't know, haven't experienced, or can't imagine doing is an opportunity for God to show us who he is and what he can do. You can joyfully praise your Father that he is pleased to do this!

- Where is it easy to lean on your own wisdom or learning?
- How has God revealed himself in your childlike faith?

Prayer Prompt: Praise God for everything he does in and through you.

# Don't Miss That!

**"Blessed are the eyes that see what you see."**
LUKE 10:23 NIV

After publicly praising his Father, Jesus privately turned to his disciples to tell them what he didn't want them to miss. They were not only seeing God's plan of salvation unfold, but they were also seeing the one through whom it was accomplished. No doubt, Jesus' words would play on repeat as they went into all the world making disciples of every nation.

Though we don't see Jesus in the flesh, we do see him in the Word. We are blessed to see our salvation completed by Christ on the cross, God working in the lives of his people, and glimpses of the glory waiting for us in heaven.

Don't miss that.

In the Word, Jesus calls us to faith through the Holy Spirit to receive every spiritual blessing, to put on the armor of God against the devil's schemes, to rejoice in suffering as participants with Christ, to be his witnesses to the end of the earth, and so much more.

Don't miss that.

Jesus is privately giving us front-row seats to see what he will do to bring glory to his name in every aspect of life around us.

Don't miss that.

"Blessed are the eyes that see what you see"!

- Assess your time in the Word. Can you level up?
- Schedule a Day Alone with God (a D.A.W.G. day)!

Prayer Prompt: Ask God for a renewed heart of appreciation for his Word.

# What Is to Come

**"Many prophets and kings wanted to see what you see but did not see it, and to hear what you hear but did not hear it."**

LUKE 10:24 NIV

Jesus continues to help the disciples realize their unique blessing. For generations, prophets and kings longed for the fulfillment of God's promises. Without understanding how it would happen or what it would look like, they trusted that God would keep his word. They *needed* him to. They knew they were sinners and experienced the impact of sin. They needed a Savior—of course they wanted to see and hear salvation with their own eyes and ears!

It's easy to relate to the disciples as we see sin touch every aspect of our lives as well. Every day we long for something better. Despair would be understandable, except we confidently know this isn't all there is. In the perfection of heaven, we will see and hear what the disciples experienced in person: Jesus.

Until then, let's live like we know that. Let the forward gaze of what is to come fill our speech and drive our actions. Let the expectancy that God will do what he promises override our disappointment in any circumstance. And let the longing for something better make us want to see and hear only Jesus.

- What makes it difficult to focus on what is to come?
- What do you expect that God is doing in your life?

Prayer Prompt: Confess your complaints about today.

# The Bad Guys

❖

**"A man was going down from Jerusalem to Jericho, when he was attacked by robbers. They stripped him of his clothes, beat him and went away, leaving him half dead."**

LUKE 10:30 NIV

Jesus told the story of the Good Samaritan to teach people that God's grace is for everyone.

A Jewish traveler was stripped, beaten, and left to die. Two different men on the road saw him but kept walking. The first was a priest; the second, a Levite. Both men were respected and esteemed religious dignitaries. The Jewish priests represented God and mediated on behalf of God's people. They preached about God's faithful love and the importance of love for neighbors. The Levites were holy men of honorable lineage who served as assistants in the temple.

Yet neither one showed compassion for their dying countryman. They passed by on the other side of the road and ignored God's command to help their neighbor. They chose the safe side. They knew that helping those in need can be complicated, costly, or time-consuming. Even messy.

Jesus knew their hypocrisy.

He knows the hypocrisy in your heart too. He died to pay for humanity's sinful thoughts, lack of compassion, and unwillingness to love others more than self.

Everyone is a bad guy. Everyone needs Jesus, the Savior from sin.

- Is it hard to see yourself as the priest or Levite?
- What acts of love might seem risky to you?

Prayer Prompt: Confess the times when you've failed to love others the way you should.

# Good Story, Good Guy

❖

**"[The Samaritan] went to him and bandaged his wounds. . . .Then he put the man on his own donkey, brought him to an inn and took care of him. The next day he took out two denarii and gave them to the innkeeper. 'Look after him,' he said, 'and when I return, I will reimburse you for any extra expense you may have.'"**

LUKE 10:34-35 NIV

Jesus continued the story of the Good Samaritan by explaining that a third man came by—and he was a Samaritan.

Up to this point, the listeners would have been caught up with compassion for the Jewish traveler and been concerned about who would help. However, as Jesus unfolded the story, kindness from a Samaritan was not the ending they wanted. The selfless love and willing generosity of this man would have been shocking. Racial hatred between the Jews and Samaritans had brewed for centuries. Their hostility was unmistakable. This could not be right! Many Jews responded angrily whenever Jesus announced that grace was for everyone.

Their attitude reflects the sin that separates us from God, but Jesus addressed their contempt and taught them that God's forgiveness is for everyone. He proclaimed that God's Son would pay the debt of sin because God loved the world.

- List the ways that Jesus is like the Samaritan.
- Imagine this story happening today.

Prayer Prompt: Ask for a heart of unbounded love that shares the true story of Jesus with others.

# Come In!

**As Jesus and his disciples were on their way, he came to a village where a woman named Martha opened her home to him.**

LUKE 10:38 NIV

Jesus traveled extensively—teaching, healing, and feeding thousands along the way. Even when exhausted, he pressed on to share God's mercy, love, and forgiveness.

In this account, Martha offers hospitality, refreshment, and rest to Jesus. She invites him in with kindness and the best of intentions. Jesus enters, knowing he will need to correct, forgive, and teach this woman who lovingly serves him.

Jesus also invites you into this story.

Come in. Come with your love for Christ, your good intentions, and your desire to serve him. Come to this familiar scene: Christ is present, you want to live by faith, and there are things that need to be done. See the opportunities to love, serve, and use your gifts for God's glory. Do your best to choose wisely.

But also know this: Like Martha, you will fail. Even with the best intentions. Even with Jesus in your heart. This account is written to give you hope and encouragement. It shows you Jesus, the forgiving and beloved Savior who wants to strengthen you with his Word.

Spend time with him and listen.

- What do you think Jesus would want to say to you?
- Describe or create an area in your home where you can spend time with Jesus.

Prayer Prompt: Confess the times when your devotions have been displaced by daily responsibilities.

# *Don't You Care?*

❖

**[Martha] had a sister called Mary, who sat at the Lord's feet listening to what he said. But Martha was distracted by all the preparations that had to be made. She came to him and asked, "Lord, don't you care that my sister has left me to do the work by myself? Tell her to help me!"**

LUKE 10:39-40 NIV

Martha isn't the bad sister. She loves Jesus! Yet she neglects his teaching, busily serving him rather than learning from him. Jesus wants Martha to know that what he gives her is more important than anything she could give him.

And where are you? At his feet receiving grace or distracted as you busily fulfill your responsibilities and callings? Reflect on this question often.

Then Martha bursts, "Don't you care?"

I'm not surprised. I have whispered the same accusation in an emergency room. I have shouted it with tears in overwhelming grief. It has racked my body in times of despair. Yes, we are also in this story as we demand and expect solutions we can see and understand.

And where is Jesus? With us. He listens as we pour out ugly thoughts, sinful accusations, and pitiful solutions. He sees our repentant hearts, wraps us in grace, and seals our forgiveness with nail-pierced hands.

- Who do you blame?
- What does it look like when worship and service are out of balance?

Prayer Prompt: Confess the times when you've said, "Don't you care?" Praise God for forgiveness.

# *What One Thing?*

❖

**"Martha, Martha, you are worried and upset about many things, but one thing is needed. In fact, Mary has chosen that better part, which will not be taken away from her."**

LUKE 10:41-42 EHV

Listen to the response of Jesus, the compassionate and gracious Savior, slow to anger and abounding in love: "You are worried and upset about many things." Rather than rightfully condemning Martha, Jesus gently acknowledges the struggles of this life. His kindness leads her to repentance, and she graciously receives his forgiveness and correction. As a poignant testimony of her growth and humility, Martha will serve dinner to her Savior again just days before he dies.

Be drawn in by your Savior's grace, understanding, and forgiveness. Receive his kindness.

Grateful hearts wait with bated breath for Jesus' next words. What now? Will he tell us to try harder? Should we promise to do better? No, certainly not.

Jesus points us to "one thing." His response is not meant to be a simple, one-word answer. As with many profound answers in Scripture, we can only marvel at our boundless God, barely grasping his infinite majesty. Here too we simply take a deep breath. We embrace his eternal and indivisible blessings: grace, forgiveness, salvation, the gospel, faith in Christ, and the Word with its powerful sacraments.

One thing is needed, and Jesus purchased it for you.

- Reflect on the importance of receiving God's forgiveness.
- List the blessings you receive from your one true God.

Prayer Prompt: Praise him for "one thing."

# The Need for Prayer

❖

**On another occasion, Jesus was praying in a certain place. When he finished, one of his disciples said to him, "Lord, teach us to pray, just as John also taught his disciples."**

LUKE 11:1 EHV

Jesus was a magnificent man of prayer. Many times, the disciples saw Jesus stop whatever he was doing and go to his Father in prayer. He prayed at meals, when he was tired, when he was sad, when he healed someone, and on many other occasions. They wanted to know the secret. How should they pray?

It might sound strange that John had taught his followers to pray but Jesus had not taught his disciples to pray. Jesus certainly prayed with them, but his ministry was different from John's. John pointed toward Jesus, the Messiah, by teaching his followers to repent and to fast and pray with sorrow over their sin and a desire for forgiveness. When Jesus began his ministry, he talked about the kingdom of God and his role in God's plan of salvation. Jesus certainly wanted his disciples to pray, but as he pointed out in Luke 5:34, "You cannot make the attendants of the bridegroom fast while the bridegroom is with them, can you?" Nevertheless, Jesus taught them to pray in preparation for being without him.

- Make a list of instances in the Bible when Jesus prayed.
- When can people see your example of being a faithful woman of prayer?

Prayer Prompt: Ask the Holy Spirit to teach your heart to pray in all situations.

# Father

**[Jesus] said to them,
"When you pray, say, 'Our Father in heaven,
hallowed be your name. Your kingdom come.
Your will be done on earth as it is in heaven.'"**

LUKE 11:2 EHV

"Our Father." What beautiful words! Jesus calls God *our* Father—yours, mine, and his! Because Jesus paid for the sin that our Father could not abide, we are part of the family. We can speak to our Father with confidence and trust.

In the next phrase, we *hallow* God, or "show respect and admiration for him." Then we ask that God's kingdom, his spiritual work on earth, come to us. Next, we pray, "Your will be done on earth as it is in heaven." These two requests fit well together. It is certainly God's will that his kingdom, his saving power, should come to us. Asking for God's kingdom to come implies that we'd like to help in the work God is doing, to be part of spreading his gospel.

While using these exact words in our prayers is fine, it is also good to use them as a starting point for more specific petitions. We may ask for help in living lives that show God's awesomeness. And since we want our words and actions to bring glory to God, we might request specific opportunities to be part of bringing his kingdom to more people.

- How can you hallow God's name?
- Do you eagerly participate in spreading the gospel?

Prayer Prompt: Ask God to help you hallow his name.

# All Our Needs

❖

**"Give us each day our daily bread."**

LUKE 11:3 EHV

Give us bread, God. It's a simple request, isn't it? We ask God for bread, but there is so much more to this petition. Here the word *bread* is a figure of speech called a synecdoche (sin-NECK-doe-key), in which a part represents the whole. So when Jesus says we should ask for bread, he is telling us to ask our Father for everything we need each day: food, shelter, clothing, and even mental health and the love of friends and family. The best part of this request is that we already know it will be answered because "God will fully supply [our] every need" (Philippians 4:19).

Using the Lord's Prayer in our daily devotions or at church may lead us to add some specifics to this petition. Our loving Father wants us to pour our hearts out to him in prayer. If, on this particular day, we need strength to face a difficult meeting at work, funds to pay an overdue bill, or a babysitter for the children, we can ask—and our Father hears.

- What requests for bread do you want to pour out to God today?
- How many items can you put on a gratitude list today?

Prayer Prompt: Thank your loving Father for supplying all your needs. Ask for the wisdom to know the difference between wants and needs.

# Deliver Us

❖

**"Forgive us our sins,**
**as we also forgive everyone who sins against us.**
**And lead us not into temptation,**
**but deliver us from evil."**

LUKE 11:4 EHV

This is the confession part of the prayer, where we humbly ask God to grant us mercy for all the wrongs we have done. It is also an acknowledgment that God expects us to forgive others because he forgives the myriad sins we have and continue to commit. Our gratitude leads us to forgive others. If specific sins bother our consciences, we can list them here and rid our souls of guilt over them. If we are struggling to forgive others, we can use this prayer to ask for help.

Finally, we ask God to watch over us and to keep the devil at bay. The Lord certainly will not lead us into anything evil, but with this petition, we ask him to protect us from our own sinful desires and the temptations of the world. We ask him to lead our feet toward his love and righteousness. What a comfort to be delivered—rescued—from evil!

- Can you use this prayer as the beginning of a conversation with God asking him to help you forgive someone?
- What does it mean to be delivered from evil?

Prayer Prompt: Confess specific sins to God. Thank Jesus for making forgiveness possible.

# BACK TO JESUS' POPULARITY

## *Luke chapter 11*

# BACK TO JESUS' POPULARITY

Luke chapter 11

*Jesus, as we look again at your time of popularity, we hear you urging people to see their need for a Savior. We hear your message today and know we need you. May the light of your love always remind us of your completed sacrifice for sin. Amen.*

# Do You Need a Sign?

**As the crowds were increasing, he began to say, "This generation is an evil generation. It is seeking a sign, but no sign will be given to it except the sign of Jonah."**
LUKE 11:29 EHV

Jesus called the crowds of his day evil because they wanted signs and miracles. They demanded proof that he was the promised Messiah. But Jesus didn't give in to the crowds. Jesus prophesied his own resurrection and called it "the sign of Jonah" because Jonah was in the belly of a great fish for three days. The resurrection of Jesus on the third day would announce his victory over sin, death, and the devil. Jesus' resurrection is the miraculous proof that God's plan of salvation is complete.

The people of the world today still want a God who will give them what they want.

And some days, we do too.

Maybe you worked hard and expect that God will arrange for a promotion at work, protect you from hardship, or make your relationships perfect. Are these the signs of God's love you look for? Jesus says that his resurrection is the sign. He has risen to assure you that grace, forgiveness, and eternal life are yours. Trust his resurrection as the sign.

- What sinful expectations undermine your trust in Jesus?
- Why does Jesus point you only to his resurrection to prove he is the Savior?

Prayer Prompt: Confess the times when you question God. Thank him for his resurrection.

# Is Your Flashlight On?

**"No one lights a lamp and puts it in a place where it will be hidden, or under a bowl. Instead they put it on its stand, so that those who come in may see the light."**

LUKE 11:33 NIV

"Siri, turn flashlight off." I was at the airport and didn't realize that the flashlight on my phone was on. A young woman came over to let me know, and I thanked her profusely. Later, I thought about these words of Jesus and wished the light of my faith would shine as brightly as my phone.

Jesus says that our purpose is to shine with his truth, love, and grace. In a sinful, dark, and needy world, our loving acts of kindness and words of truth can point people to see the light of free salvation and forgiveness in Christ.

If only it were that easy.

I was embarrassed that my flashlight was on and fumbled to turn it off. Do you ever feel that way about your faith? Are you nervous that someone might notice your light? It's okay. Believers often struggle with awkwardness, but Jesus doesn't want you to be hidden. Jesus put you in a specific place and shines through you to draw others to himself.

"Jesus, turn flashlight on."

- In what ways do you shine your light?
- How could you respond to those who see your light and appreciate your kindness?

Prayer Prompt: Ask for strength and wisdom to share God's love.

# Bad Eyes

**"Your eye is the lamp of the body.
When your eye is good, your whole body is full of light.
But when it is bad, your body is full of darkness."**
LUKE 11:34 EHV

Jesus frequently talks about light as he explains spiritual life. With eyes of faith fixed on Jesus, believers are filled with his light, love, and joy. At the same time, Jesus also gives a stern warning about darkness, and these words are equally important: "When [your eye] is bad, your body is full of darkness." Jesus' words are clear. When you soak up the darkness of sin, your life is dark. Bad eyes glance at sin with desire. Bad eyes linger in darkness with a sinful imagination. Bad eyes stare as sin becomes full-blown evil.

These words of Jesus are for you. Jesus fills you with his light, but he knows the temptations of darkness. He knows exactly what happens when your eyes go bad. With perfect love, he warns you. Better yet, Jesus conquered the darkness and won the victory over sin. Jesus' death and resurrection secured the gift of forgiveness for you. Be warned of sin's dangerous consequences. But even more, trust his light that has overcome darkness and shines on you with grace.

- Where do your eyes wander?
- Where do your eyes soak up the light of Jesus?

Prayer Prompt: Ask for wisdom to see the dangers of darkness and for strength to live in the light of forgiveness.

# Dirty Dishes

**"You Pharisees clean the outside of the cup and dish, but inside you are full of greed and wickedness."**

LUKE 11:39 NIV

Jesus was having dinner at the home of a Pharisee when he spoke these sharp words. The Pharisee invited Jesus to dinner and then watched him carefully. He wondered if Jesus would keep the extra laws written by the religious leaders to make themselves look good. But Jesus saw right through this hypocrisy. Jesus knew this Pharisee harbored pride and self-righteousness in his heart. And Jesus called him out very clearly.

Everyone likes to look good on the outside, but Jesus looks on the inside. The grit in the glasses when the dishwasher is done reminds you that being clean on the outside isn't clean enough. God demands that his people are perfectly clean—inside and out. Obeying the law can never make you clean enough. Instead of trying harder to look clean, you can trust in Jesus your Savior to wash away all your sin and unrighteousness. These sharp words of Jesus speak to you when you try to look good by your outward behavior. They remind you that you need a Savior. Thank God you're cleansed by Jesus!

- What does Jesus' sharp tone teach you about the seriousness of sin?
- Are you ever tempted to think that a little grit doesn't matter?

Prayer Prompt: Confess the times when you've been tempted to feel righteous because of what you've done. Thank God for his cleansing blood.

# JESUS' FINAL MONTHS

*Luke chapters 12-18*

# JESUS' FINAL MONTHS

Luke chapters 12-18

*Holy Christ, Son of God, we watch as your sacrifice to pay for the sins of the world approaches. Strengthen us to hear the truth of your words and urgent warnings. Fix our eyes on you as you go to the cross to complete your work of salvation for us. Amen.*

# What Are You Really Worth?

**"Are not five sparrows sold for two pennies?
Yet not one of them is forgotten by God.
Indeed, the very hairs of your head are all numbered.
Don't be afraid; you are worth more than many sparrows."**
LUKE 12:6-7 NIV

It is hard to stay balanced and rest securely in the value given to us by Jesus.

Sometimes we fall into despair, overwhelmed by our failures and shortcomings. All we can think of is what we do wrong or what we can't do at all. We feel worthless. Other times, arrogance drives us to pursue goals with our own strength and skill. Selfish motivation pushes us toward success. The end justifies the means—and we feel prideful.

But grace and truth place us, perfectly balanced, in the nail-pierced hands of Jesus, where we can rest.

Knowing how much Jesus values us, we are free from the despair of failure. Our sins are covered by Jesus. Things that aren't going well are used by him to shape our character or to bless others. Our personal goals and the development of our skills are motivated by grace and thankfulness, and we pursue them for his glory.

Need to see it more clearly? Look at the cross. See the dying body of God's Son to know your worth. Your value is unquestionable, and God's love is unfathomable.

- What if God's value doesn't feel like enough?
- How can you fight feelings of unworthiness?

Prayer Prompt: Ask God to give you peace as you see your value to him.

# Know Any Rich Fools?

**"[The rich fool] said,
'This is what I'll do. I will tear down my barns
and build bigger ones, and there I will store my surplus grain.
And I'll say to myself, "You have plenty of grain laid up
for many years. Take life easy; eat, drink and be merry."'
But God said to him
'You fool! This very night your life will be demanded from you.
Then who will get what you have prepared for yourself?'"**

LUKE 12:18-20 NIV

I don't have barns full of wealth, but I know I don't live up to what Jesus is teaching here. I'd like to think that if I had this much money, I would look for ways to help other people. Jesus' love moves me to serve others and put their needs ahead of my own . . . at least on some days.

Here Jesus teaches us that life is not about possessions. He warns against greed. Our goal in life should not be to eat, drink, and be merry. But left to our own thinking, it would be. This parable urges us to consider how much we value money and how we plan to use it. We need to repent when we are selfish and greedy.

Then we remember that Jesus forgives these sins too.

- In what ways does money tempt you to sin?
- Will those who receive your inheritance be on guard against greed?

Prayer Prompt: Confess the times when you are like the rich fool. Ask God to guard your heart against greed.

# The Kadupul Blossom

❖

**"Consider how the wild flowers grow.
They do not labor or spin. Yet I tell you, not even
Solomon in all his splendor was dressed like one of these.
If that is how God clothes the grass of the field,
which is here today, and tomorrow is thrown into the fire,
how much more will he clothe you—you of little faith!"**

LUKE 12:27-28 NIV

Sri Lanka's Kadupul flower is considered priceless to some because it lives only a few hours after it is picked. It blooms for a little while around midnight and releases a lovely fragrance, but people rarely see it.

Why would God place a beautiful, fragrant cactus blossom on an island off the coast of India to bloom when most people are sleeping? Because the Creator loves beauty and is glorified by the wonders of nature. And if God watches over this flower in a unique place with an aroma and beauty that only a few people might briefly enjoy, how much more will he care for you?

God's beautiful earth was marred by sin that separated God from his people. Then God sent Jesus to pay our debt of sin and restore our relationship with him because his loving care is perfect.

- How are Christians like the Kadupul blossom?
- What has God clothed you with, and what is your aroma?

Prayer Prompt: Thank God for making you a beautiful, aromatic blossom that glorifies him even in the darkness of this world.

# Be Watchful

**"It will be good for those servants whose master finds them watching when he comes. Truly I tell you, he will dress himself to serve . . . and will come and wait on them."**

LUKE 12:37 NIV

Smudged fingerprints on the living room window, children with eyes glued to the driveway—these are just some of the characteristics of children who are watching and waiting for their grandparents to arrive.

You are called to watch for your Savior in the same way. But watchfulness doesn't mean sitting idle. Instead, it looks like being a parent, going to work, praying with others and showing love to them, and eagerly embracing the Christian life in every way.

And when Jesus returns to find you watching, what will he do? He will serve and wait on you! "Look, I am coming soon! My reward is with me" (Revelation 22:12). Because the one who washed his disciples' feet and gave his life "as a ransom for many" (Matthew 20:28) will bring you the reward of salvation and an eternal home.

As you wait for Jesus to return, be watchful and carry out your responsibilities with faithfulness because he promises more than just a reunion—he promises an eternity with him.

- In what ways are you watching for Jesus to return?
- How can you serve others out of thankfulness for God's forgiveness in Christ?

Prayer Prompt: Praise Jesus for his humility not only to serve you but also to be your Savior from sin.

# Christ Alone

**"Do you think I came to bring peace on earth? No, I tell you, but division."**

LUKE 12:51 NIV

We often order our priorities in a way that we think will bring us earthly peace, but Scripture reminds us that there is one priority above all others, and it often brings something far from peace in this life.

Not only are our priorities important to us as they apply to our personal wellness, family, and future, but they are also important to our Savior.

God sets us on a path of salvation that will test our priorities again and again. We face division and difficulty throughout our journey, and these obstacles are nothing short of reminders to prioritize Christ, and Christ alone.

Sadly, we will fall short again and again as we face these challenges. But we can be joyfully confident that our Savior is committed to our success! He purchased and won us from the punishment of sin. The challenges, and even the failures, are opportunities for refinement. God calls us to a glorious purpose and belonging in his kingdom, and he will not break his promise of salvation. The beauty is that the peace of Christ, the hope of heaven, and our secured salvation help us keep the goal of earthly peace in its proper perspective.

- When have you prioritized the pursuit of earthly peace over Christ?
- How can you check your priorities when life's challenges come?

Prayer Prompt: Ask God for perseverance in trials and "Christ alone" priorities.

# Asking the Best Question

❖

**"Do you think that these Galileans were worse sinners . . . because they suffered this way? I tell you, no! But unless you repent, you too will all perish."**

LUKE 13:2-3 NIV

You've seen it on the news before. A tragic accident takes its toll on humanity, sadly ending the lives of many and causing great heartache. When bad things like this happen, the question to ask isn't "Why did God allow that to happen?" or "What sort of people were they to deserve that?"

Jesus teaches you to ask the best question: "Are you ready if something like that were to happen to you?" He uses these tragedies to emphasize a harsh reality: "The wages of sin is death" (Romans 6:23). No one is exempt from sin and death, but death is not the end for those who believe.

Jesus gives you a personal and urgent call to repent because the last thing he wants is for death to have the final say in your life. God says, "I take no pleasure in the death of the wicked, but rather that they turn from their ways and live" (Ezekiel 33:11).

To repentant hearts, death is but the gateway to eternal life with him.

- Are you harboring sins that keep you from readiness?
- What can you say to someone who needs to hear the call to repent?

Prayer Prompt: Praise God for calling you to repentance and granting forgiveness to all who believe.

# Free to Praise

❖

**When Jesus saw her, he . . . said to her, "Woman, you are set free from your infirmity." Then he put his hands on her, and immediately she straightened up and praised God.**

LUKE 13:12-13 NIV

What image comes to mind when you hear the word *free?* A carefree child running around the backyard on a summer day? A day to relax and do absolutely nothing?

For the woman in this story, her life was anything but free as she had been crippled by an evil spirit for 18 years. But when Jesus saw her, he reached out in compassion and gave her a life of freedom. It only took a few words and a single touch, and immediately she was healed. And the result? Praise for God!

The greatest freedom she received, however, was the forgiveness of sins. A life of true freedom is one that has been released from the bondage of sin. Because of God's mercy, this woman received physical and spiritual healing. You too are free "to offer your bodies as a living sacrifice, holy and pleasing to God—this is your true and proper worship" (Romans 12:1).

You're set free to praise him.

- What images in your daily life remind you of the freedom Jesus gives?
- How can you embrace a life of true freedom?

Prayer Prompt: Praise God for giving you true freedom to live for him.

# Free to Rest

❖

**"Doesn't each of you on the Sabbath untie your ox or donkey from the stall and lead it out to give it water? Then should not this woman . . . be set free on the Sabbath day from what bound her?"**

LUKE 13:15-16 NIV

Jesus gave true freedom to a woman who was crippled for 18 years, and the immediate result was praise and thanksgiving to God. This miracle occurred on the Sabbath, a day God ordained and set aside for rest.

Instead of praising God with this woman for her healing, the religious leaders were bent out of shape. They made their customs about rest more important than the reason for which God gave the Sabbath in the first place. The Sabbath was never supposed to be a day that bound people with restrictions and laws. Rather, it was meant to be a day of freedom to find rest and celebrate God's goodness.

Some days, you might find yourself getting bent out of shape for the wrong reasons, but remember God's good purpose is always to give you rest in him.

And just as the woman was set free from her infirmity, you're also set free from sin to rest in your Savior.

- What things take away from the rest God wants you to have?
- How can you celebrate God's gift of rest?

Prayer Prompt: Confess when you've gotten bent out of shape for the wrong reasons. Ask God to focus you on spiritual rest.

# Yeast

**"To what will I compare the kingdom of God? It is like yeast, which a woman took and mixed into a bushel of flour until it was all leavened."**

LUKE 13:20-21 EHV

In these verses, Jesus is telling us about himself and his kingdom on earth. To help us understand, he uses metaphors. The kingdom of God, the creation of saving faith in the souls of God's people, spreads like yeast. It only takes a little bit of God's love to affect a huge number of people and help them rise. His love is such abundance!

It's hard to know if *bushel* is the best word for the amount of flour Jesus was talking about because we don't use the same measurements today, but it sounds like a huge amount, doesn't it? Imagine the difficult but fulfilling work of mixing yeast into an entire bushel of flour, watching the dough rise, baking the bread, and feeding many people! What joy!

And what joy to be used by our Lord to mix his yeast into the lives of people around us, to share the Word of God that brings salvation. The Holy Spirit's work is both simple and powerful, and it changes hearts just like yeast changes flour.

- How can you share God's yeast?
- Why do you think Jesus used this comparison of yeast and flour to describe his kingdom?

Prayer Prompt: Praise Jesus for bringing his kingdom to our lives.

# Narrow Door

**"Strive to enter through the narrow door, because many, I tell you, will try to enter and will not be able."**
LUKE 13:24 EHV

Just before this verse, Jesus was asked, "Are only a few going to be saved?" (Luke 13:23). Jesus didn't answer the question directly, but he did tell everyone how to get to heaven. The word *strive* might seem to indicate that Jesus was telling his listeners to do something or to try to earn their salvation, but that is not the case. Instead, Jesus was encouraging people to focus on the way to heaven, the "door" he would open when he died on the cross to pay for sin. The door is called "narrow" because it is the only way to eternal life. There is no other way.

The best part of Jesus' answer is that he opens the door. Faith in him is the only way—the only door to heaven. Those trying to enter heaven through their own merit or actions will be left out, but those who walk through the open door of faith in Jesus' sacrifice will be with him forever. So the number of people is not the issue. The way of salvation is the issue—and that way is Jesus, our door.

- How do you strive to enter the narrow door, and how can your faith be strengthened?
- Do you ever wonder how many people will be in heaven?

Prayer Prompt: Thank Jesus for being the door to heaven.

# People Will Come

**"People will come from east and west, from north and south, and will recline at the table in the kingdom of God."**

LUKE 13:29 EHV

These words were a warning to the religious leaders in Jerusalem that their standing with God did not depend on their outward adherence to laws and traditions but, rather, on faith in Jesus as their Savior from sin.

And these words are also an invitation to us.

Jesus opens heaven to the people of the world.

With this verse, Jesus says he has come to save the whole world, and all who believe in him will spend eternity at the Lord's banquet in heaven.

The concept of reclining at a table may be unfamiliar to us, but the feeling of acceptance and love is universal. An invitation to share a meal and conversation means we are considered family or friends. The person inviting us desires our company. And all of us are invited. We will not all look, sound, or act the same, but we will all be welcomed around God's table because he has invited us, dwells with us, and will bring us to his home. Imagine reclining around God's table with people from all over the world!

- Do you think this warning to the religious leaders of Jesus' time is a warning that Christians need today?
- Who can you invite to dinner as an opportunity to share Jesus' love?

Prayer Prompt: Thank God for your invitation to his table in the kingdom!

# I Longed to Gather You

❖

**"Jerusalem, Jerusalem, the city that kills the prophets and stones those sent to her! How often I have wanted to gather your children together, as a hen gathers her chicks under her wings, but you were not willing!"**

LUKE 13:34 EHV

As women, many of us can relate to the maternal instinct that desires to love and protect the children around us: our own children, family members, church members, or our friends' children. Thinking of Jesus as a hen gathering up chicks is a little bit funny until we put ourselves in the place of those chicks and realize that Jesus longed to love, protect, and cherish those who wanted him dead. Even more, Jesus was willing to die for the sins of all people so he could gather them in his arms for eternity.

Jesus' words were directed toward his Father's chosen people, the line of people through whom he had been born, yet they refused to recognize him. So many prophecies had been fulfilled. So many times God had sent prophets to tell his people what to expect, what to do, and what to believe. But the people didn't believe it when they saw it. Jesus wanted to love them, but they were unwilling to accept his love.

- Which prophets did Jerusalem kill?
- Is it difficult for you to willingly be gathered up by Jesus?

Prayer Prompt: Confess the times when you've been unwilling to listen to God's Word. Thank Jesus for his loving protection.

# He Who Humbles Himself

**"All those who exalt themselves will be humbled, and those who humble themselves will be exalted."**

LUKE 14:11 NIV

Jesus was eating dinner at the house of a prominent religious leader when he noticed how the dinner guests were seating themselves. Seeing a teachable moment, he told them a parable about humility and being exalted.

In the parable, Jesus gave the example of a wedding feast. He explained that it would not be wise for a person to assume a position of high esteem in the eyes of the host. Seating oneself in a place of honor and being asked to move down would be an embarrassment, but seating oneself in a place of low esteem and being asked to move up would be a great honor.

So it is in the kingdom of heaven. Those who seek esteem in the eyes of the world but do not honor the ways of God will one day find that they are not esteemed at all before the Lord. However, those who are humble in spirit—serving others and seeking the will of the Lord—will be exalted in the kingdom of heaven.

Praise Jesus that he was willing to be humbled as our Savior so we could receive God's invitation to the eternal banquet of heaven.

- How do people exalt themselves?
- How did Jesus demonstrate humility and service?

Prayer Prompt: Ask God to guide you to seek his will and to give you a spirit to serve.

# Declining the Greatest Invitation

❖

**"A certain man was preparing a great banquet and invited many guests. At the time of the banquet he sent his servant to tell those who had been invited, 'Come, for everything is now ready.' But they all alike began to make excuses."**

LUKE 14:16-18 NIV

Jesus told parables to teach the truths of God's Word. He told this parable about a great banquet while he was at a dinner in a Pharisee's home. A man unexpectedly expressed a genuine longing for the heavenly banquet, so Jesus told this story. Jesus showed how God first offered his invitation to his chosen people, the Jews.

In the parable, the original invitation went out and had been accepted. Then the servant told the guests that the banquet was ready. Though the time had come, the original guests decided they had more important things to do.

The Jews had received and accepted the original invitation to enjoy a place of honor in God's kingdom, but when Jesus arrived to tell them the time had come, many had misplaced priorities and declined.

Today as well, many reject God's invitation of forgiveness in Christ. Excuses keep them from enjoying God's blessings now and will prevent their presence at the heavenly banquet in eternity.

- What excuses do people make to avoid time with God?
- Can you think of a time when you declined an invitation from God?

Prayer Prompt: Ask God to forgive you for not putting his invitation first in your life.

# Attending the Great Banquet

❖

**"Then the master told his servant, 'Go out to the roads and country lanes and compel them to come in, so that my house will be full. I tell you, not one of those who were invited will get a taste of my banquet.'"**

LUKE 14:23-24 NIV

The parable continued after the original guests made excuses. The master of the banquet sent his servant to invite "the poor, the crippled, the blind and the lame" (Luke 14:21). The servant did this, and there was still room. The master did not discriminate. He wanted every person to receive an invitation and his banquet to be filled to the brim.

The invitation to the original guests would no longer be extended, however. It was too late for them.

When the Jews rejected Jesus, the invitation to salvation was taken away from them and given to the Gentiles. The news of forgiveness in Christ was spread far and wide: in the cities, the countryside, and across all nations.

God's invitation is for all people; he wants heaven to be filled with people from all nations. He wants us to enjoy the blessings that come with the invitation to trust Christ's work on the cross both now and for eternity.

- What blessings come with the invitation to God's heavenly banquet?
- Is there someone you could invite to the banquet in heaven?

Prayer Prompt: Praise God there is a place in heaven for every person who receives his invitation.

# The Real Cost

❖

**Large crowds were traveling with Jesus, and turning to them he said: "If anyone comes to me and does not hate father and mother, wife and children, brothers and sisters—yes, even their own life—such a person cannot be my disciple. And whoever does not carry their cross and follow me cannot be my disciple."**

LUKE 14:25-27 NIV

On the surface, this hard statement seems contrary to everything else Jesus teaches, which is a clue that we need to dig deeper.

Jesus speaks of the real cost of discipleship. He does not want leftover love or attention only when things are difficult; he wants our whole heart. He wants a love so deep that it permeates every part of our life. He wants a devotion so complete that the love we have for others looks like hate in comparison to our love for him.

Jesus does not sugarcoat the real cost of following him. He says there will be difficulties in true discipleship. The people understood the picture of carrying one's own cross—it was the final thing they would ever do. To carry our cross means to wholeheartedly follow Jesus even when it's hard or if it's the last thing we do.

But first, we must always remember the cross he carried, which completed our salvation.

- What does love for Jesus look like?
- What difficulties have you faced in following Jesus?

Prayer Prompt: Ask Jesus to help you carry the cross of true discipleship.

# Building Expenses

**"Suppose one of you wants to build a tower. Won't you first sit down and estimate the cost to see if you have enough money to complete it?"**

LUKE 14:28 NIV

Have you ever done a home renovation project? A general contractor I worked with once told me to take our best estimate and multiply it by 3 to get a truly accurate idea of the total cost. As a carpenter, Jesus knew the power of a good construction analogy.

In these verses, Jesus encourages his followers to consider everything that is included in building a Christian life. Much like the parable of the sower, where some seeds wither because the roots aren't deep, our understanding of building expenses is an important part of our Christian growth.

The materials are expensive, even more than we think they will be. But bear in mind, these godly life-building materials are well worth the cost. Our supply list includes rare and precious items like humility, self-control, a servant's heart, patience, and gentleness. Anyone with these qualities will tell you that they don't arrive via same-day delivery. They come as a gift from God and the fruit of the Spirit's work.

As you consider the cost, remember the investment God made in you. Jesus purchased you with his blood, and now he is building you into his master plan.

- Are you feeling the strain of building expenses?
- What Bible verse can you repeat to remind yourself that God is your builder?

Prayer Prompt: Ask God for wisdom for today's building projects.

# Waging War and Winning

❖

**"Won't [a king] first sit down and consider whether he is able with ten thousand men to oppose the one coming against him with twenty thousand?"**

LUKE 14:31 NIV

I'm not great at poker. People who excel at that game are unusually talented at separating their thoughts and feelings from their facial expressions and body language. That's not something I'm sure I can fully comprehend, let alone attempt.

However, there is another strategy I'm aware of that's much more possible for those of us who wear our heart on our sleeve. If you want to win at playing poker, you need to play your opponent, not your cards.

Jesus talked about our faith commitment in terms of war. He pointed out how, before going to war, a king will first consider not only his own arsenal but also his enemy's strength. As followers of Christ, we will encounter war. We are being relentlessly pursued by the devil, sin, and death. Know your opponent.

Do you know what will get us a win? Jesus says the only way to certain victory is to trust *his* victory over our opponent. Jesus won the great, eternal battle over the devil, sin, and death for us.

- Where do you feel most susceptible to the enemy's schemes?
- What or who are you holding on to as protection instead of leaning wholly on God?

Prayer Prompt: Confess the times when you depend on earthly sources of comfort or strength for the battle.

# That's Gross

❖

**"Salt is good, but if it loses its saltiness . . . it is fit neither for the soil nor for the manure pile."**

LUKE 14:34-35 NIV

If you have boys in your life—if you raise them, teach them, coach them, befriend them, date or marry one, etc.—you understand the power of gross. The higher the disgust factor of an idea, the more intrigued most boys will be. And, honestly, I get it. Gross things elicit powerful smells, sights, and feelings. They are hard to forget.

With this in mind, I'm going to gross you out for a second.

Did you know that prior to refrigerators, salt was used to preserve meat? Salt was (and still is) excellent at preventing the growth of dangerous bacteria. It's also fantastic at—here's the gross part—keeping maggots away from meat.

As Christians, Jesus commands us to live a salty life: a life seasoned and preserved by the gospel.

A woman who invests consistent, intentional time in the Bible carries life-giving, maggot-preventing power within her to share with the world. Her saltiness can sprinkle Jesus' hope, joy, power, and peace on everyone in her path.

If we aren't living a salty life, we're wasting a tremendous resource. Now *that's* gross.

- What Bible verse makes you feel extra salty?
- Who might need a sprinkle of your God-given salt today?

Prayer Prompt: Thank God for giving us his words of truth for protection and purpose.

# Greener Pastures

**"Suppose one of you has a hundred sheep and loses one of them. Doesn't he leave the ninety-nine in the open country and go after the lost sheep until he finds it?"**

LUKE 15:4 NIV

The grass is always greener on the other side. This phrase is commonly used when other people's lives or situations seem better than your own. You don't need to look far to see how others are doing. They seem to have it all—the perfect house, the perfect job, the perfect family. Isn't it easy to fall into the temptation of wanting what you don't have?

Just like sheep searching for greener pastures, it's easy to wander from the flock in search of things that you think will make you happier. These things can quickly turn into idols that make you lose focus and become lost in the world.

Yet you have a Shepherd who relentlessly seeks to find you and bring you safely home. He doesn't need you to be perfect. In fact, he knows you won't be. His love is greater than all the times you fail. His forgiveness extends to you time and time again because he died on the cross for your sins.

What a relief to know you are found!

- Are you ever tempted to let perfectionism get in the way of being content with what you have?
- What might you say to someone who is wandering or lost?

Prayer Prompt: Thank God for his forgiveness when you've been tempted to wander from your Shepherd.

# A Reason to Rejoice

❖

**"Or suppose a woman has ten silver coins and loses one. . . . When she finds it, she calls her friends and neighbors together and says, 'Rejoice with me; I have found my lost coin.'"**

LUKE 15:8-9 NIV

When was the last time you lost something valuable? Maybe it was years ago, or maybe it just happened yesterday. How did it make you feel? I imagine you felt stressed or worried and urgently wanted to find what was lost.

After searching tirelessly, you find it—what joy and relief you feel! Certainly, it's personal joy, especially if the item held sentimental or monetary value. But how much more joy would you feel if it holds spiritual value?

Your soul is of utmost value to God. When you were lost in sin, Jesus, the pioneer and perfecter of your faith, "for the joy set before him . . . endured the cross" (Hebrews 12:2). He took it upon himself to make you his own. That's the kind of value God places on you.

The joy of a faith found and secured in God cannot compare to anything on this earth. It's a reason for rejoicing and a reason worth sharing.

- How can you share your reason for rejoicing with others?
- In what ways can you live in this newfound joy?

Prayer Prompt: Ask for courage and urgency to share your reason for rejoicing with others.

# The Prodigal Son

❖

**"This son of mine was dead and is alive again; he was lost and is found."**

LUKE 15:24 NIV

In this famous parable, Jesus sets the scene between a rebellious son and a patient father. The son requests his share of the father's inheritance, basically wishing his father was dead, and then goes off and spends it all—how reckless!

Unfortunately, you share those same reckless behaviors when you think you can handle life on your own terms. Not seeing a relationship with God as important or not caring about the consequences of sin makes you lost. And in God's eyes, it makes you spiritually dead.

Yet in spite of your rebellious nature, your heavenly Father does an amazing thing: he waits patiently for you to come to your senses. He does everything he can to bring you back home. And when you return, he welcomes you with open arms!

Just as the son received a welcome he did not deserve, you also receive God's compassion and forgiveness. You were once spiritually dead, but because of God's love for you, you are now spiritually alive in Christ.

- What behaviors tend to lead you down a reckless path?
- How might you show forgiveness to someone who rebels against you?

Prayer Prompt: Ask God to help you come to your senses when you rebel against him. Thank him for showing compassion and forgiveness.

# The Other Prodigal Son

**"Meanwhile, the older son was in the field. When he came near the house, he heard music and dancing. The older brother became angry and refused to go in. So his father went out and pleaded with him."**

LUKE 15:25,28 NIV

Where the younger son in Jesus' parable was reckless and selfish, the older son was dutiful, responsible, and faithful to his father. A picture of perfect obedience. Yet it becomes obvious that he was just as lost as his brother.

Instead of joining in the welcome feast when he learns of his brother's return, the older son is angry and resentful. How dare his father forgive someone so reckless, so foolish!

Just like the older son, it is easy to resent God's gracious forgiveness of someone you criticize to be a far worse sinner than yourself.

If you find yourself in the same situation as the older son, God still pleads for you to return to him. And because of his only Son, forgiveness is yours too. Don't let anything keep you from sharing that joy of forgiveness and peace with others.

- When do you find it hard to forgive others?
- How can you share the peace of forgiveness with someone who needs it?

Prayer Prompt: Confess to God when you fall short of showing forgiveness to others.

# The Father's Love

❖

**"'My son,' the father said, 'you are always with me,
and everything I have is yours.
But we had to celebrate and be glad,
because this brother of yours was dead and is alive again;
he was lost and is found.'"**

LUKE 15:31-32 NIV

Throughout this parable, you've seen how both sons were lost in their ways. Yet both share a father who shows patience, compassion, and forgiveness despite their actions against him.

Each day you sin against your heavenly Father, yet each day he shows you grace. How amazing and undeserved! But some see this behavior as reckless. What kind of God keeps showing love to sinners despite their many faults?

In a way, God could be seen as prodigal. The word *prodigal* means "wastefully or recklessly extravagant, giving or yielding profusely."

God is recklessly extravagant in that he spent everything on you. He sent his one and only Son to die so that you might live. His love reaches out to sinners like you no matter why or how you got lost. What an amazing Father you have!

- What does God's forgiving love look like in your life?
- How specifically could you show grace and love to those the Father is seeking?

Prayer Prompt: Praise God for being recklessly extravagant in his love for you each day.

# The Check Mark of Faithfulness

❖

**"The person who is faithful with very little is also faithful with much. And the person who is unrighteous with very little is also unrighteous with much."**

LUKE 16:10 EHV

Too often, I try to fit things into clearly defined boxes emphasized with bold lines. I want life's experiences to go into one box or another.

When I hear Jesus' words in this text, I want to put a check mark in the faithful box. Honestly, I want to fill it in with a permanent marker right up to the edges. I want to be faithful. I want to use my gifts, opportunities, and time to share the love of Christ. I know I've been entrusted with the message of the gospel, and I want to do the right thing!

With my next breath, I know I've failed. I know I need Jesus to remove the check mark of my unrighteousness with his blood. I need him to fill in the box of *my* faithfulness with *his* faithfulness.

Praise God he did.

Renewed, I pray to be faithful for his glory. I may fall short, but I am forever compelled by the love of Christ to continue in grace. I pray to be found faithful as a steward of my entire life because my box is already checked and filled in, right up to the edges, by Jesus.

- When is it hard to be faithful?
- What if you are unrighteous in little things?

Prayer Prompt: Praise Jesus for his faithfulness.

# Why God Is Our Master

❖

**"No one can serve two masters."**

LUKE 16:13 NIV

As our Creator, God formed us from the dust and gave us breath. He allows us to bear his image. That makes him our Master.

As our Father, he calls us to be his loving children. He urges us to bring our needs and concerns to him. That makes him our Master.

As our Savior, he gave his life so that we would no longer be slaves to sin. Instead, we are slaves of his righteousness. That makes him our Master.

As our Holy Spirit, he provides us with spiritual food and lives within us. He shows us why and how to live. That makes him our Master.

As our King, he provides justice and protection. He rules over us for our good. That makes him our Master.

As our Prince of Peace, he has conquered sin, death, and the devil. He reigns victoriously. That makes him our Master.

As our Shepherd, he watches over us, knowing our every need. He leads us to good pastures and quiet waters. That makes him our Master.

- Why is it difficult sometimes to acknowledge and yield to God as your Master?
- How can your life give witness to the blessings of a loving Master?

Prayer Prompt: Praise God for his majesty, holiness, and authority. Thank him for being the Master who loves us and gave himself for us. Ask for opportunities to talk about the blessings of being under his care.

# He Is Comforted

❖

**"Abraham replied, 'Son, remember that in your lifetime you received your good things, while Lazarus received bad things, but now he is comforted here and you are in agony.'"**

LUKE 16:25 NIV

Jesus told a parable about a beggar named Lazarus who lay at the gate of a very wealthy man. Lazarus longed to eat the scraps from the man's table, but the rich man was selfish and had no compassion. Even the stray dogs showed more kindness to Lazarus as they licked his wounds.

Both men died.

From hell, the rich man could see Lazarus in heaven with Abraham, so he called out, pleading for a drop of water to soothe his anguish. Abraham reminded the man of the riches he had selfishly treasured on earth. And because the man had no faith, he was eternally condemned by his sin.

Lazarus was received into the glories of heaven by faith. Christ has paid the debt of all sin, and those who trust in him have eternal life. Though believers suffer with hardships in this life, God promises eternal life filled with holiness, peace, and joy.

- How does this parable give comfort to believers who are struggling or hurting?
- Think of people you know who don't realize they need Jesus. How can you help them?

Prayer Prompt: Ask God to help you see those who need him despite outward appearances. Confess the times that you are lukewarm in your love for the lost.

# Let Them Listen

❖

**"[The rich man] answered, 'Then I beg you, [Abraham], send Lazarus to my family, for I have five brothers. Let him warn them, so that they will not also come to this place of torment.' [Abraham] said to [the rich man], 'If they do not listen to Moses and the Prophets, they will not be convinced even if someone rises from the dead.'"**

LUKE 16:27-28,31 NIV

The rich man begs for his brothers to be saved and spared from eternal anguish in hell. "Send Lazarus!" he pleads. Surely, they would listen to a man who comes back from the dead!

But God's plan to save people from sin is delivered through his Word. When Abraham says "listen," it implies faith and trust in Jesus, the promised Messiah, for forgiveness and salvation. God creates, nurtures, and strengthens faith only through the Word. He does not send new messages through ghosts, dreams, or revelations.

Abraham's reply reminds us of Romans 10:17: "Faith comes from hearing the message, and the message is heard through the word about Christ."

As Jesus said, "Whoever has ears, let them hear" (Matthew 11:15).

- How can you show love to people who do not listen to the Word?
- Describe the urgency of telling others about Jesus.

Prayer Prompt: Ask God for opportunities to share Christ's salvation with others through the message of the Word. Praise him for the power of the Word!

# Protect Others From Stumbling

**"Things that cause people to stumble are bound to come, but woe to anyone through whom they come."**

LUKE 17:1 NIV

Picture an evening when parents ask their teen to babysit a younger sibling while they go out. The children intended to behave, but upon returning, the parents find that the children got into trouble. Turning to the teen, they say, "You should have known better!"

Unfortunately, sin happens even if you have the best intentions to be good.

What a comforting truth we can run to when we have sinned—we have forgiveness because Christ died to pay for sin! We rest in God's mercy, and we also hear the warning Jesus gives in this text: Do not cause others to continue in sin because it is harmful to their souls.

It is your duty to protect fellow Christians from stumbling, just as the teen had a duty to watch over a younger sibling. Even more than parents with a duty and plan to protect their children, God has a plan to protect his family—and it includes you! God calls believers to watch out for one another and warns them against causing others to sin. This responsibility has the eternal good of others in mind.

- How might you be causing a fellow Christian to stumble?
- How could you keep your spiritual siblings from stumbling?

Prayer Prompt: Ask God for strength and wisdom when situations arise that could cause others to sin.

# Forgiveness Restores

❖

**"So watch yourselves. If your brother or sister sins against you, rebuke them; and if they repent, forgive them."**

LUKE 17:3 NIV

A gut punch to the stomach. Feelings like emptiness, pain, and even anger. These are symptoms of realizing someone has sinned against you. And they hurt.

It's inevitable that people will sin, and specifically, against you. But rather than harboring bad feelings against them or making them go through a guilt trip for the pain they caused, Jesus gives you two steps to follow: rebuke them, and if they repent, forgive.

To *rebuke* doesn't mean to point out every sin you see like an accountant keeping a record of wrongs. Rather, it means to bring sin to a person's attention with the purpose of restoring a believer to God and other people.

One petition of the Lord's Prayer says it plainly, "Forgive us our sins, just as we also have forgiven those who sin against us" (Matthew 6:12 NIRV). By resting in God's promises and basking in the freedom of forgiveness that you enjoy every day, you have the strength to forgive, especially those who have sinned against you.

- How might you forgive in times when it would be easier to get back at those who hurt you?
- What promises can you give to someone who repents?

Prayer Prompt: Praise God that his forgiveness restores you and others to the family of believers.

# Faith Like a Mustard Seed

**The apostles said to the Lord, "Increase our faith!" He replied, "If you have faith as small as a mustard seed, you can say to this mulberry tree, 'Be uprooted and planted in the sea,' and it will obey you."**

LUKE 17:5-6 NIV

Consider for a moment the tasks before you this week, month, or year. Do any of them seem unattainable? Often, it's easy to feel inadequate about the tasks before you.

The disciples felt the same way when they received Jesus' command to forgive others. Essentially, they cried in response, "Our faith is too small. Give us more!" But they missed the point.

Instead of focusing on the strength of their faith, which by itself can do nothing, Jesus points them—and you—to the strength of what faith holds on to: God. With your faith firmly planted in God and his promises, you can be confident that he will provide for all your needs.

You may think that your faith is the size of a mustard seed, but take comfort in this: The size of your faith is not the focus but, rather, the object to which it is attached. Your faith is in an extraordinary God!

- Which tasks are weighing you down that you can take to God?
- In what ways can you exercise your living and active faith?

Prayer Prompt: Thank God for the faith he's worked in your heart to be able to do his will.

# Take Up Your Duty With Joy

❖

**"So you also, when you have done everything you were told to do, should say, 'We are unworthy servants; we have only done our duty.'"**

LUKE 17:10 NIV

A general gives orders to his soldiers, and they obey without question. You take your pets to obedience classes so they obey your commands. In both cases, it's their duty to obey.

In the same way, it is your duty to obey God's will—to love, serve, and forgive others. Obedience to God is not something optional or extra that you do to earn his favor. When by God's grace you *are* able to do what he commands, don't let your pride get the better of you to think that you did those things by your own power!

Our obedience to God is only possible because of Christ's death on the cross. His death and resurrection now enable us to live for God in service to others. God is more than capable of doing everything by himself, yet he chooses us for meaningful service. Obeying him is a privilege! It's not done to earn anything. Rather, we obey out of humble thanks. And that is a duty we take up with joy.

- How might your pride get in the way of service to others?
- In what ways can you serve joyfully?

Prayer Prompt: Thank God that you have nothing to earn, since he earned it all for you. Ask him to give you opportunities to serve others joyfully.

# Ten Lepers

**One of [the lepers], when he saw that he was healed, turned back, glorifying God with a loud voice. He fell on his face at Jesus' feet, thanking him. And he was a Samaritan.**

LUKE 17:15-16 EHV

I want to be like this leper! Sins healed, I want to be the one "glorifying God with a loud voice." But am I one of the nine, going off to celebrate and forgetting to praise God?

Jesus and his disciples were headed to Jerusalem (Jesus would soon die to save these ten—and us). Ten lepers called out, "Jesus, Master, have mercy on us!" (Luke 17:13). Jesus told them to go show themselves to the priests, a necessary step for a person to rejoin society. The healing began as they walked, and it is understandable that they did not want to turn around.

Yet one returned, and he was a Samaritan. We assume the other nine were Jews, who should have thought to be thankful. Jesus told the one, "Your faith has saved you" (Luke 17:19). It was important for the disciples to see this encounter because it showed them that Jesus came for all people, not just the Jews. We also know and are thankful that our faith saves us.

- When have you cried out to Jesus for his mercy?
- Why is it important that Jesus told a foreigner his faith had saved him?

Prayer Prompt: Glorify God in a loud voice for his healing power in your life.

# When Jesus Appears

❖

**"It will be the same on the day the Son of Man is revealed. On that day, the person who is on the roof and has belongings in the house should not go down to get them. Likewise, the person in the field should not turn back for anything. Remember Lot's wife! Whoever tries to preserve his life will lose it, but whoever loses his life will keep it."**

LUKE 17:30-33 EHV

The disciples were confused about the kingdom of God, what it was and when it would come. Jesus pointed them ahead to the day he would return in glory. He told the disciples not to chase after sightings of him because he will come like lightning, illuminating the entire sky. No one will miss it. He compared his coming to the flood of Noah's time and the destruction of Sodom in the days of Lot. In these instances, Noah and Lot trusted God and his plan and were saved. But most people went about living their daily lives with no faith in God, and they perished. Lot's wife looked back, wanting to cling to her life a bit longer. It did not end well for her.

Jesus made it clear to his disciples, and to all believers, that putting our hope in this life will not end well. But putting aside our love for this life and clinging by faith to Jesus will lead to life with him in his eternal kingdom.

- What sinful desires of this life cause you to look back?
- How can this promise from Jesus comfort us when we face our final moments on earth?

Prayer Prompt: Ask God for a faith that looks forward to eternal life and does not cling to earthly life.

# The Persistent Widow

**Jesus told them a parable about the need to always pray and not lose heart.**

LUKE 18:1 EHV

In this parable, a persistent widow continually pleaded with a local judge for justice from her adversary. Was she just a nagging, annoying woman? The unjust judge thought so. Jesus says he "did not fear God and did not care about people" (Luke 18:2). He granted her justice only because he wanted her to go away and leave him alone.

On the contrary, God is just and *does* care about people.

In Luke 18:7-8, Jesus asks, "Will not God give justice to his chosen ones, who are crying out to him day and night?" He continues by answering his own question: "I tell you that he will give them justice quickly." As God's people, we can pray confidently and continually, knowing God loves us and sent his Son to die for us. Since God met our greatest need in Christ, we can be sure he hears our many prayers.

Jesus continues, "When the Son of Man comes, will he find faith on the earth?" (Luke 18:8).

Praise God! Because of Christ's sacrifice for sin, he will find faith on the earth in us!

- Do you ever feel like you are nagging God if you say the same prayer numerous times?
- What does this parable teach about God?

Prayer Prompt: Ask the Spirit to deepen your desire to pray and increase your trust that God will answer your prayers.

# The Pharisee and the Tax Collector

❖

**"I tell you, this man went home justified rather than the other, because everyone who exalts himself will be humbled, but the one who humbles himself will be exalted."**

LUKE 18:14 EHV

The parable of the Pharisee and the tax collector is familiar. The Pharisee praised himself, shouting his adherence to laws as if he had earned his way into God's favor. The tax collector, who had committed many sins, begged for forgiveness.

It might be tempting to think the Pharisee's biggest issue was his public proclamation. Surely, no one we know would stand before the congregation proclaiming his or her greatness. But Luke 18:9 says, "Jesus told this parable to certain people who trusted in themselves (that they were righteous) and looked down on others." It wasn't just about outward arrogance; it was about where our trust lies.

It can be tempting to think, "I teach Sunday school, plan events, and donate money; surely, God is pleased with me." Pharisee! Then, to be humble, should I put all my sins out there so others see how God has forgiven me? No. The tax collector "stood at a distance" (Luke 18:13). In the end, this story encourages us to study God's Word to be reminded of our depravity and God's mercy.

- In what ways do you identify with the Pharisee?
- In what ways do you identify with the tax collector?

Prayer Prompt: Join with the tax collector in confessing your sins and asking God for his mercy.

# Such as These

❖

**Jesus called the children to him and said, "Let the little children come to me, and do not hinder them, for the kingdom of God belongs to such as these."**

LUKE 18:16 NIV

Children often touch a soft spot in our hearts and move us to feelings of warmth or kindness. Sweet faces, funny actions, and cute comments are endearing. We can imagine Jesus tenderly saying, "The kingdom of God belongs to such as these."

But Jesus isn't talking about loving bonds with children or the joys they bring. He is correcting his disciples and teaching them how people enter the kingdom of God—with humble trust like children.

The word translated "little children" appears often in Scripture and refers to infants, young children, and, in some places, immature believers. Like all people, they are covered by God's grace and forgiveness. They bring nothing. Only those who trust in the completed work of Christ as the payment for their debt of sin will enter God's kingdom.

This truth shines brightly in God's Sacrament of Holy Baptism as sin is washed away in even the tiniest hearts. Cleansed by water and the Word, we all look to Christ for our solid hope of heaven.

- In what ways does an infant's dependence or helplessness reflect what Jesus was teaching?
- How does your life reflect the heart of a trusting child who eagerly learns and accepts truth?

Prayer Prompt: Ask God to strengthen your trust in him.

# *Who Can Be Saved?*

**A certain ruler asked him,**
**"Good teacher, what must I do to inherit eternal life?"**
LUKE 18:18 NIV

Jesus' preaching drew many people to see their sin and trust him as the promised Savior. Many embraced his teaching—but not all.

One day, a self-righteous ruler came to Jesus and asked what he must do to be saved. Jesus answered him with a summary of the commandments. Jesus wanted him to see his need for a Savior; instead, the man replied, "All these I have kept since I was a boy" (Luke 18:21). Jesus saw the man's prideful heart. Knowing that the ruler loved his wealth, Jesus commanded him to sell everything he had and give to the poor. Jesus longed for the man to see his spiritual need and trust God's plan for salvation. The man walked away from Jesus—he loved his money more than anything else.

May we reply with trust in Christ whenever the commands of God reveal our need for a Savior.

In Luke 18:24-25, Jesus adds a final warning, "How hard it is for the rich to enter the kingdom of God! Indeed, it is easier for a camel to go through the eye of a needle than for someone who is rich to enter the kingdom of God."

- How do you know what you treasure most?
- What is Jesus' simple point about the camel and the needle?

Prayer Prompt: Ask God to guard your heart against self-righteousness.

# HE COMPLETES OUR SALVATION

*Luke chapters 18-24*

# HE COMPLETES OUR SALVATION

Luke chapters 18-24

*Lord God, the pinnacle of the gospel accounts is the unfathomable mystery that you sent your Son to die for sinners. Every moment, every word, and every event in this account has been recorded for your glory and our good. We praise you. Amen.*

# Everything Written

**"Everything that is written by the prophets about the Son of Man will be fulfilled. He will be delivered over to the Gentiles. They will mock him, . . . flog him and kill him. On the third day he will rise again."**

LUKE 18:31-33 NIV

The Word of God includes more than three hundred prophecies about Jesus, and it also shows us that every prophecy was fulfilled. Mathematicians use symbols to represent the astronomical unlikelihood that all these prophecies could be fulfilled. It's miraculous. Only God could accomplish it. And he did.

As Jesus and his disciples made their final trip to Jerusalem to celebrate the Passover, Jesus explained what would happen. Of course, it is clear to us. With heartache, we can visualize the mocking, beatings, and crucifixion that Christ would endure.

But the disciples had none of those images in their minds. Because they couldn't comprehend what Jesus was telling them, they weren't prepared for the horror, the cruelty, and hours of bloody torture when it unfolded before them.

Then the disciples saw the resurrected Savior with their own eyes.

We can't imagine the Lord's resurrection glory as seen by the disciples. But someday, we too will stand in his presence and behold his glory.

- What prophecies can you remember?
- Would you rather be a 21st-century Christian who knows the full story or a 1st-century disciple who personally saw it unfold in real life?

Prayer Prompt: Praise God for fulfilling all prophecy!

**Those who led the way rebuked [the blind man] and told him to be quiet, but he shouted all the more, "Son of David, have mercy on me!" Jesus stopped and ordered the man to be brought to him. When he came near, Jesus asked him, "What do you want me to do for you?" "Lord, I want to see," he replied. Jesus said to him, "Receive your sight; your faith has healed you."**

LUKE 18:39-42 NIV

This account is often called The Blind Beggar Receives Sight, but it's much deeper than a joyous day for a blind man.

By persistently calling Jesus the "Son of David," the blind beggar was demonstrating that he already had sight. His sight was not physical, but spiritual.

The beggar had previously heard of Jesus' authoritative teachings and miraculous healings. Word about the Savior had traveled through the countryside, and now the man could hear an unusually large crowd moving through his area.

As he shouted out, he was shouted down. He knew this was his chance, so he persisted.

When Jesus healed, he would often provide spiritual healing first and then physical healing. Here he simply healed with physical sight because he could see that the man's heart already held saving faith; his soul already knew its forgiveness.

- How would a beggar's life change after receiving physical sight?
- How is your life changed because of spiritual sight?

Prayer Prompt: Thank God for spiritual and physical blessings.

# Zacchaeus

❖

**Zacchaeus stood up and said to the Lord, "Look, Lord! Here and now I give half of my possessions to the poor, and if I have cheated anybody out of anything, I will pay back four times the amount." Jesus said to him, "Today salvation has come to this house, because this man, too, is a son of Abraham. For the Son of Man came to seek and to save the lost."**

LUKE 19:8-10 NIV

Zacchaeus was despised by his fellow Jews. He was a chief tax collector for the Romans, living a life of excess while cheating his neighbors.

Because of his short stature, Zacchaeus had to climb a tree to get a glimpse of Jesus—something that would have been terribly embarrassing for someone of his position. When Jesus announced he would be staying with Zacchaeus, many questioned Jesus' desire to be in the company of sinners.

Yet Zacchaeus was overjoyed with Jesus' visit. He invited friends to dinner and willingly gave back more than what would be expected. His newfound generosity was a response to the grace and forgiveness of Jesus. The salvation he found in Jesus prompted him to say, "Look, Lord!" just like an excited child would say to a father. Zacchaeus had been lost in sin, but Jesus sought him out of the crowd and saved him.

- What had Zacchaeus loved more than God?
- How can you respond to Jesus' grace?

Prayer Prompt: Thank Jesus for seeking and saving you.

# The Minas Are Given

❖

**"A man of noble birth went to a distant country to have himself appointed king and then to return. So he called ten of his servants and gave them ten minas. 'Put this money to work,' he said, 'until I come back.'"**

LUKE 19:12-13 NIV

It was nearing the time of the Passover, which meant the Jewish people heading to Jerusalem were feeling an increased sense of nationalism. They still had misplaced notions about the role of Jesus and surely thought they were marching into the city with the one who would free them from the Roman occupation. The parable Jesus told was to focus them on the real intent of his mission.

In the parable, the appointed king is Jesus. His ministry was coming to an end, and he would soon depart for heaven, where he would be crowned with all authority in heaven and on earth. The servants who were given a treasure of minas represent Jesus' followers, then and now, who have been entrusted with a precious treasure—the gospel.

We are to put the gospel to work, sharing God's Word with souls near and far. One day, Jesus will come back and call to account all those he entrusted with his gospel.

- What was the real intent of Jesus' pilgrimage to Jerusalem?
- How can you put the gospel to work in your life?

Prayer Prompt: Ask the Lord to help you be faithful in sharing his gospel with others.

# The Minas Accounted For

❖

**"The first one came and said, 'Sir, your mina has earned ten more.' 'Well done, my good servant!' his master replied. 'Because you have been trustworthy in a very small matter, take charge of ten cities.' The second came and said, 'Sir, your mina has earned five more.' His master answered, 'You take charge of five cities.' Then another servant came and said, 'Sir, here is your mina; I have kept it laid away in a piece of cloth. I was afraid of you, because you are a hard man.'"**

LUKE 19:16-21 NIV

When the appointed king returned, he called his servants to account for the minas he had left them. He was pleased with those who had invested his treasure, and he found them to be trustworthy stewards. The lazy, frightened servant who hid his treasure away, though, was met with anger for squandering his opportunity.

Jesus wants us to be like the faithful servants: putting his treasured gospel to work and having it come back to him multiplied and bearing much fruit in the lives of others. When the day comes to give an account, our Savior's perfect life and innocent death will ensure that we hear, "Well done, my good servant!" Knowing this, we strive to be faithful stewards of the gospel out of thankfulness for Jesus.

- Which servant do you relate to?
- Have you ever thought of the gospel as a treasure?

Prayer Prompt: Ask God to multiply the gospel.

# The Lord Needs It

❖

**"If anyone asks you, 'Why are you untying it?' say, 'The Lord needs it.'"**

LUKE 19:31 NIV

Do you ever feel like God is asking you to do something really strange or difficult? Maybe it's befriending someone whose personality just doesn't make sense to you. Or it could be navigating a chronic illness in yourself or a loved one. For some of us, it's joyfully embracing a season (or two or three) of singleness.

I bet the disciples felt like Jesus asked them to do a lot of strange things. One good example of this happened on the day we recognize as Palm Sunday. Before Jesus rides into Jerusalem, he sends two disciples on a mission to go acquire a colt (young male donkey) for him to ride on. He doesn't explain to the disciples why he needs it. In fact, the only explanation he offers for anyone at all in this whole donkey adventure is "The Lord needs it."

What if that's all the reason God ever gave you? Would that be enough for you?

Be that weird person's friend because the Lord needs it. Carry yourself with an attitude of gratitude despite your chronic pain because the Lord needs it. Be contentedly single because the Lord needs it.

Because God is perfect, we know that his need doesn't point to a deficiency.

- What does *need* mean?
- What obstacles are keeping you from doing what the Lord needs?

Prayer Prompt: Praise God for his eternal perspective of need.

# A Stone's Cry

❖

**"If they keep quiet, the stones will cry out."**

LUKE 19:40 NIV

For as long as I can remember, my favorite quote from the great C. S. Lewis has been from his book *Miracles*. He says, "Miracles do not, in fact, break the laws of nature." For me, this statement says just as much about nature as it does about miracles.

The more you understand about nature, the more complex and incredible it becomes. Did you know some particles of sand are actually microscopic seashells? Or how about snow—have you ever seen how uniquely and delicately designed each flake is? And how on earth do birds know exactly when and where to migrate?!

As Jesus rode into Jerusalem on Palm Sunday, the crowds chanted and cheered in celebration of their King. The Pharisees' reaction was to tell Jesus to quiet his disciples. And Jesus told the Pharisees, "If they keep quiet, the stones will cry out."

I know Jesus could've very literally made the stones nearby shout his praises, but their very existence already glorified their Maker. Think about it: There's a reason Christ is known as our cornerstone.

- What characteristics of nature bring a sense of awe and wonder to your understanding of God?
- How do stones silently glorify God?

Prayer Prompt: Celebrate God today, as the disciples (and rocks) did on Palm Sunday, for his miraculous ways, his mercy-soaked salvation, and his role as King in our lives.

# Jerusalem Moments

❖

**As [Jesus] approached Jerusalem and saw the city, he wept over it and said, "If you, even you, had only known on this day what would bring you peace."**

LUKE 19:41-42 NIV

Only three verses in Scripture speak about Jesus crying during his time here on earth. John 11:35 tells us that "Jesus wept" when Lazarus died, and Hebrews 5:7 speaks in general about the times in Jesus' life when he "offered up prayers and petitions with fervent cries and tears." The third reference is from Luke's gospel where Jesus weeps for Jerusalem and says, "If you . . . had only known."

Jesus' weeping over the city's stubborn rejection of its Savior shows how full of mercy and love he is. Jesus knows the pain we feel over our personal moments of rebellion against him. He weeps with us over our loved ones' rejection and the future it leads to. He felt the weight of that sorrow and sacrificed his life anyway. This is the kind of love he taught us.

I have also said these very words.

They are incredibly gut-wrenching. Every time I've used them, they've been soaked with grief over how simple, beautiful, or comfortable a situation could have been instead of the present painful reality.

- When have you personally known the grief of "if you . . . had only known"?
- How does Jesus' response to Jerusalem impact your expression of love today?

Prayer Prompt: Thank God for peace despite our Jerusalem moments.

# A Different Kind of Mad

**"It is written," [Jesus] said to them,**
**"'My house will be a house of prayer';**
**but you have made it 'a den of robbers.'"**
LUKE 19:46 NIV

This one is for all my sisters who struggle with a short fuse. I do too. And if you're like me, not everything is a trigger. But there are some things that just immediately engage frustration level 10 (e.g., when the kiddos hear the plan for the day and then ask, "What are we doing today?" 30 seconds later).

Jesus had a much better (perfect) internal monitor on his fuse. The disciples asked the same question all the time, and he never seemed to tire of reminding them who he was and why he came. We don't hear about any signs of frustration over people trying to trap him into sinning. He didn't get annoyed by a constant barrage of people wanting healing and help from him.

But one thing did get to him. Twice in his life, he chased people out of the temple with a bold display of righteous anger. Why? Because people were making the temple—a place specifically set aside to purposefully worship God and offer sacrifices—into a source of earthly distraction.

- Is church the only place where earthly distractions keep you from a heavenly focus?
- What things help you stay focused on Jesus at home?

Prayer Prompt: Ask God to align your emotions with his today.

# Whose Authority?

❖

**"Tell us by what authority you are doing these things."**

LUKE 20:2 NIV

Jesus' teaching challenged the religious leaders and contradicted their self-righteous preaching. His message of love angered them. But many people who had come for the Passover still gathered around Jesus in the temple courtyard. The people marveled at his words and were drawn to his tender forgiveness. Jesus spoke with authority, unlike the chief priests and teachers of the law.

After a Passover celebration almost 20 years earlier, the chief priests and teachers of the law had marveled at the questions asked by a 12-year-old boy. They had listened in awe of his understanding and answers. But now Jesus was grown—and he posed a threat to their false teaching and empty security. And they were no longer interested in the truth. They only wanted to hear what soothed their itching ears and barren souls. The further they drifted from the Word, the harder their hearts became.

They didn't believe Jesus' words: "The Father . . . commanded me to say all that I have spoken" (John 12:49). They refused his truth: "I do not speak on my own authority. Rather, it is the Father, living in me" (John 14:10). They didn't hear the Father proclaim, "This is my Son, . . . listen to him" (Luke 9:35).

- Do you think any teachers in Jerusalem remembered Jesus as a young boy? Why do you think that?
- What other Scripture affirms Jesus' authority?

Prayer Prompt: Ask God to humble you under his authority.

# The Evil Tenants

❖

**"A man planted a vineyard, rented it to some farmers and went away for a long time. At harvest time he sent a servant to the tenants so they would give him some of the fruit of the vineyard. But the tenants beat him and sent him away empty-handed."**

LUKE 20:9-10 NIV

Jesus told this parable in the temple courtyard on Tuesday of Holy Week.

On Friday he would pay for the sins of all people with his blood—even the sins of the evil tenants.

Here is the parable: A man (God) planted a vineyard, put a wall around it, erected a watchtower to protect it, and built a winepress in eager anticipation of the sweet fruit that would grow in his vineyard (Mark 12:1). Nothing was left undone. The owner entrusted its care to farmers, or tenants, who were chosen for a gracious opportunity to oversee and nurture the land.

But the farmers forgot about the owner and his gifts. Pride took root in their hearts and choked their faith. When the owner sent his servants for a portion of the fruit, they were flogged.

The Jewish leaders had rejected God's prophets and message of mercy. God wanted his vineyard to flourish, but sin destroyed the relationship God had with his farmers—and his relationship with us.

- Was Jesus only condemning the sin of the religious leaders?
- How did God save the vineyard for eternity?

Prayer Prompt: Thank God for the spiritual farmers who nurture faith.

# The Son Is Sent

**"Then the owner of the vineyard said, 'What shall I do? I will send my son, whom I love; perhaps they will respect him.' But when the tenants saw him, they talked the matter over. 'This is the heir,' they said. 'Let's kill him, and the inheritance will be ours.' So they threw him out of the vineyard and killed him. What then will the owner of the vineyard do to them? He will come and kill those tenants and give the vineyard to others."**

LUKE 20:13-16 NIV

Jesus' message is poignantly clear. The Jewish leaders would kill the Son of God and be eternally condemned. The vineyard would be given to others.

Jesus knew the Jews were plotting to kill him. His accusation was unmistakable, and the religious leaders heard his judgment—so did the crowd.

What Jesus said came true. The death of the only Son brought forgiveness, and when he died for sin, he opened the vineyard to all who call on his name.

Now God works in the vineyard as he plants his Word in hearts through Baptism, protects us with Scripture as an unfailing watchman, and gives us the Holy Supper to strengthen our faith and bear fruit.

- How is your calling as a Christian like a farmer?
- Do you know a gardener who would be blessed to hear this story about God's loving care?

Prayer Prompt: Ask God to bless his vineyard with good fruit.

# What's the Real Question?

**"Is it right for us to pay taxes to Caesar or not?"**

LUKE 20:22 NIV

Yes, people grumbled about paying taxes two thousand years ago.

Taxes reminded the Jews they were under Roman authority. Though they maintained quite a bit of self-righteousness and national pride, they lived under Caesar's rule.

But that's not really the conversation here.

The gospels tell us about the intention of the religious leaders who were baiting Jesus. If Jesus said, "Yes, pay taxes," he would alienate the people. If he said, "No, don't pay taxes," the religious leaders could turn him over to Rome. Either way, they thought they could ruin him.

With simplicity and brevity, Jesus gives a timeless answer as he holds out a common coin: "Give back to Caesar what is Caesar's, and to God what is God's" (Luke 20:25). Scripture affirms that God establishes government for the good of the people. Even more, it exalts the Lord, who never fails to love his people.

Jesus was never deterred from his mission. He wasn't tricked or distracted by the things of this life—he came to save sinners from death. His words give wisdom for life in this world, but Jesus himself gives us life for eternity in heaven.

- What other words of Scripture have been helpful for life in this world?
- Think of specific ways good citizenship glorifies God.

Prayer Prompt: Ask God to work through governments to bless people and maintain peace.

# The Age to Come

❖

**"The people of this age marry and are given in marriage. But those who are considered worthy of taking part in the age to come and in the resurrection from the dead will neither marry nor be given in marriage."**

LUKE 20:34-35 NIV

Think about the relationships in your life—perhaps with a spouse, parent, child, or friend. These relationships are important to you! And it's hard to imagine life without them, right?

Your relationships on earth, or "of this age," as Jesus said, are filled with amazing blessings, but even those blessings are limited by time, sin, and death. It is only in heaven, or "the age to come," where your relationships will be perfect, just as God intended them to be.

Consider how much you treasure the people in your life. Then remember that heaven will not be an extension of life as you know it now. It will be better!

That reality of eternity belongs to you because Jesus, the resurrected Savior, died on the cross to pay for your sins. He worked faith in your heart by his Holy Spirit. You can rest assured that at the end of this age, heaven is waiting for you.

- How can you make the most of your time here on earth to glorify God?
- What assurance can you give to someone who is worried about life after death?

Prayer Prompt: Ask God to fill you up with the joy of what's to come.

# True God and True Man

❖

**Jesus said to them, "Why is it said that the Messiah is the son of David?"**

LUKE 20:41 NIV

Did you ever have a "stump the teacher" day in school? Usually, it was a chance to ask the teacher a tricky question he or she wouldn't be able to answer.

The religious leaders of Jesus' day regularly tried to stump him with their questions. Now it was Jesus' turn to ask them a question—to teach them an important truth. His question got to the heart of what they believed about the Messiah's identity. How could God's Messiah be the son of David? Would he be divine or human? They didn't understand that Jesus would be both God and man, fulfilling all the prophecies written about him.

In the same way, the central question for your life is "Who is Jesus?" He is more than simply a knowledgeable teacher or the son of David as the religious leaders thought. He is your Redeemer—true God and true man.

And because Jesus is who he says he is, your faith is certain, your salvation is complete, and your hope is secure.

- What attributes of Jesus remind you that he is both true God and true man?
- What can you say to people when they ask you who Jesus is?

Prayer Prompt: Praise God that because Jesus is who he says he is, you can confidently share that good news with others.

# A New Robe

❖

**"Beware of the teachers of the law.<br>They like to walk around in flowing robes<br>and love to be greeted with respect in the marketplaces and<br>have the most important seats in the synagogues<br>and the places of honor at banquets."**

LUKE 20:46 NIV

When you got dressed this morning, how many times did you look in the mirror to make sure you looked presentable? Were you worried about how others might perceive you?

The religious leaders worried a lot about their appearances and positions. These leaders were supposed to be faithful shepherds for the people, but, unfortunately, they lost sight of their purpose and focused more on themselves than on serving others.

Think of John the Baptist. His greatest boast was not to point to himself but to Christ: "He must become greater; I must become less" (John 3:30). John's purpose was to point people to their Savior.

As a Christian, your purpose is to give glory to the God who has given you a new, marvelous robe at Christ's expense. Not a robe that boasts of yourself but a robe of righteousness that radiates the holy love of Christ who died to redeem sinners.

What a privilege to present yourself each day with his robe and love!

- How does your new robe impact the way you present yourself?
- Why don't you need to worry about your spiritual appearance before God?

Prayer Prompt: Thank God for the new robe you now get to wear because of Christ's love for you.

# *Quality, Not Quantity*

❖

**Jesus . . . saw a poor widow there putting in two small coins. He said, "Truly I tell you, this poor widow put in more than everyone, for all these put in some of their leftovers as gifts to God, but she, out of her poverty, put in all that she had to live on."**

LUKE 21:2-4 EHV

Jesus was an expert teacher. He gets his disciples' attention by saying, "Truly I tell you"—like a teacher's "Listen up," alerting the class to important information. Then Jesus contrasts two opposite ideas about offerings: the rich versus the poor.

Was his point how much to give? Certainly not. Rather, Jesus draws attention to matters of the heart.

While Jesus' lesson isn't about the amount of the offering, the widow's willingness to give all she had shows her significant trust in God's providence. Even more noteworthy than her trust is her motivation. Some were giving leftovers out of their wealth, but the widow's offering came from a heart fully devoted to her Lord.

This lesson wasn't just for the disciples. It defines the grace of giving for us today as well. Offerings that come from a devoted heart of faith are God-pleasing regardless of the amount.

- How have you been like the rich people in the temple?
- How can this text redirect the motives of your heart to grow in the grace of giving?

Prayer Prompt: Confess to the Lord the times when you have held on to part of your heart.

# Do Not Be Terrified

❖

**"Many will come in my name, saying, 'I am he,' and 'The time is near.' Do not follow them. Whenever you hear of wars and revolutions, do not be terrified, for these things must happen first, but the end will not be right then."**

LUKE 21:8-9 EHV

Jesus was teaching in the temple courts, and some people were talking about the beauty of the temple. Jesus let them know the future. This ornate temple would be destroyed, and Israel would be defeated. More important, the entire world would end.

Understandably, the disciples and the others wanted to know the signs of the end. Jesus began with a word of warning and a word of encouragement. He didn't want them, or us, to be tricked by people who claim to know the date and time of Jesus' return or claim to be the Savior. And as terrifying as "wars and revolutions" are, we shouldn't be afraid. These things need to happen, but God is still in charge. Though violence and turmoil fill the world, believers can live with confidence that Jesus will come to our rescue at the appointed time.

- What examples have you seen of people claiming "the time is near" contrary to biblical teaching?
- What are some ways to avoid being terrified when wars and violence are in the news?

Prayer Prompt: Ask the Holy Spirit for peace when you're afraid of violence on earth. Praise Jesus for his work of salvation that has secured your eternal peace.

# I Will Give You Words

❖

**"I will give you words and wisdom that none of your adversaries will be able to withstand or contradict."**

LUKE 21:15 EHV

There will be "horrifying sights and great signs from heaven" as we wait for the return of our Savior (Luke 21:11). And even before those terrible things, Christians will be persecuted—brought before government and religious leaders for trial. It happened in the time of the early Christian church, and it will continue until the Last Day.

Jesus tells his listeners to put their trust in him; he would give them the words they need to speak. That promise is true for believers today as well; that wisdom, those words, are the Scriptures. They are the words of God that we read, hear, and memorize. We don't need our own power or brilliance; we only need what God has already given us. It may be frightening and daunting to be questioned, persecuted, or suffer hardship, but with God we will prevail. Luke 21:19 tells us, "By patient endurance you will gain your lives." As we depend on Jesus' redemption, we can let the Holy Spirit speak through us. Through Christ we gain eternal life, no matter what happens in this life.

- What is the most important Bible verse you have memorized?
- How can you handle being hated for your faith?

Prayer Prompt: Thank God for providing his Word of Truth that brought you to faith and keeps your faith strong in the face of adversity.

# Lift Up Your Heads

❖

**"When these things begin to happen, stand up and lift up your heads, because your redemption is near."**

LUKE 21:28 EHV

There will be so many terrifying signs of the end of the world that people will be "fainting from fear" (Luke 21:26). Even the heavenly bodies will change, and "nations will be in anguish" (Luke 21:25). Then something will happen that will either add to the terror or bring rejoicing: "They will see the Son of Man coming in a cloud with power and great glory" (Luke 21:27).

Believers who know that Jesus lived perfectly in our place, died for our sins, rose from the dead, and ascended into heaven can do something unusual. We will stand at that moment and lift our heads with joy. These signs will not warn us that our destruction is imminent; they will be signs that our "redemption is near." And when we see Jesus coming in the clouds, we will not fear. Judgment day will not bring us terror because we have Jesus' righteousness and we know that he will take us to heaven to be with him.

- Can you imagine what it will look like when Jesus comes in a cloud?
- How can you use moments of fear as opportunities to share your faith in Jesus and your certainty of eternal life?

Prayer Prompt: Ask God to help you "stand up and lift up" your head when you see frightening signs of the earth's demise.

# Watch Yourselves

❖

**"Watch yourselves or else your hearts will be weighed down with carousing, drunkenness, and the worries of this life, and that day may come on you suddenly."**

LUKE 21:34 EHV

Watch your heart! Consider what weighs you down and what frees you. This passage comes right after the familiar words of Luke 21:33: "Heaven and earth will pass away, but my words will never pass away." Knowing this world will pass away should keep us from fixating on it, but sometimes we still do. Our pursuit of fun and fulfillment or our worries over money and prestige weigh us down and steal our joy. Even the blessings of life can weigh us down if they make us long for this life more than we long for eternal life with Jesus.

So Jesus says, "Watch yourselves." Be ready for him. How can you be ready? Focus on his words that will never fade away, his words that create and strengthen faith. Trust in his work on the cross to save sinners. And pray. Jesus tells us to pray and to cling to him so that when he comes back, we can stand before him in confidence with light and happy hearts.

- What elements of this life, good and bad, threaten to take your attention away from your faith and hope of heaven?
- What things help you keep your focus on Christ?

Prayer Prompt: Ask God to help you keep your eyes always on the cross of Christ and to protect you from being swept away by this life.

# Judas Succumbs

❖

**Then Satan entered Judas, called Iscariot, one of the Twelve. And Judas went to the chief priests and the officers of the temple guard and discussed with them how he might betray Jesus. They were delighted and agreed to give him money. He consented, and watched for an opportunity to hand Jesus over to them when no crowd was present.**

LUKE 22:3-6 NIV

Jesus came in humility to die for the sins of all people—and he was betrayed by a friend.

Judas was chosen by Jesus and trusted by the disciples, but wealth deceived him, filled him with greed, and lured him into sin. Satan entered his heart.

The religious leaders were also steeped in sin and hatred. They were livid when Jesus called out their hypocrisy, and they searched for a way to be rid of him. Now they had a way. Though Jerusalem would be overcrowded with Jews for the Passover, Judas would find the right moment to hand over and betray the Son of God.

Yet a glorious truth prevails. It was Jesus' perfect will and love for sinners that compelled him to go to the cross. Jesus wanted to save us, so he allowed himself to be betrayed. And this glorious truth also prevails: He did it for you.

- Think of ways that Satan leads people to paths of destruction.
- Have you ever considered the cost of a temptation?

Prayer Prompt: Praise God for his willingness to be your Savior.

# Preparations for the Passover

❖

**Jesus sent Peter and John, saying,**
**"Go and make preparations for us to eat the Passover. . . .**
**As you enter the city, a man carrying a jar of water will meet you.**
**Follow him . . . and say to the owner of the house,**
**'The Teacher asks: Where is the guest room, where I may**
**eat the Passover with my disciples?'**
**He will show you a large room upstairs, all furnished.**
**Make preparations there."**

LUKE 22:8,10-12 NIV

As Jesus traveled in and out of Jerusalem during his final days on earth, Judas was looking for a private moment to hand Jesus over to the Jews. But Jesus' Passover plans demonstrated that God's timing governed all things.

The preparations on Thursday included purchasing a perfect lamb, taking it to the temple to be slaughtered, and seeing the priest sprinkle its blood to atone for sin. The disciples likely returned to the house carrying the lamb bound to a pole.

Never again would they see the lamb's sacrifice without remembering what Jesus did to pay for their sin. Never again would they carry a sacrificial lamb without humility and deep reverence for their Savior.

- Think of the man who showed Jesus the room, and ask yourself, "What might God do if I open my home to others?"
- What preparations do you make to help you focus on the true reason for holiday celebrations?

Prayer Prompt: Praise the Lamb who was sacrificed for the sin of the world.

# Jesus' Eager Desire

❖

**"I have eagerly desired to eat this Passover with you before I suffer. For I tell you, I will not eat it again until it finds fulfillment in the kingdom of God."**

LUKE 22:15-16 NIV

Compelled by love, Jesus was eager to share the Passover meal with his disciples. He knew this was his last evening with them, and he longed to worship with them, to rejoice in God's unfailing faithfulness.

The Passover meal they ate reminded them of God's mighty hand as he brought his people out of slavery in Egypt. The disciples remembered the slavery of their ancestors; Jesus knew all people were slaves to sin. The disciples remembered slavery under Pharaoh; Jesus knew we were slaves under Satan. The disciples remembered their people bound in slavery for many years; Jesus knew that without his death, we would be slaves forever.

The Passover was a shadow of things to come. The "fulfillment in the kingdom of God" will be an eternal banquet and glorious celebration in heaven—a joy we cannot imagine. In eternity, we will not remember the pains of our submission to sin or slavery to death. We will gladly rejoice in the presence of our master and Savior Jesus, who eagerly desires to be with us.

- What aspects of worship do you eagerly desire the most?
- How does the Lord's Supper remind you of the banquet of heaven?

Prayer Prompt: Praise God for freeing you from slavery to sin.

# Jesus Institutes the Lord's Supper

❖

**He took bread, gave thanks and broke it, and gave it to them, saying, "This is my body given for you; do this in remembrance of me." In the same way, after the supper he took the cup, saying, "This cup is the new covenant in my blood, which is poured out for you."**

LUKE 22:19-20 NIV

Jesus and his disciples celebrated the Passover meal. They sang psalms, listened to the Word, and ate food that was rich in symbolism.

Soon Jesus would die, and God's ultimate deliverance of his people would be complete. Shadows would give way to light, and prophecies would be fulfilled. Therefore, a new promise was given: the church would grow and flourish under grace. To bless his church, Jesus established the Lord's Supper as a tangible reminder of his sacrifice and to impart his strength. We are blessed not for obeying a command or contemplating a symbol but because Jesus gave us the Supper and said, "This *is*."

Now believers eagerly gather to worship and receive food that is not symbolic but filled with the real presence of Christ. In praise to the Lord who is unfailing in his faithfulness, we receive his body and blood.

- In what ways is the Lord's Supper different from the Passover?
- List examples of Old Testament symbolism or commands that are no longer a part of the New Testament church.

Prayer Prompt: Praise Jesus for his body and blood, given for the forgiveness of sins.

# A Passover Like No Other

❖

**"Behold, the hand of him who betrays me is with me on the table. For the Son of Man goes as it has been determined, but woe to that man by whom he is betrayed!"**

LUKE 22:21-22 ESV

Jesus had given the disciples much to think about during their time in the upper room. The tradition of celebrating the Passover with immediate family had been revised to reflect a family of believers with Christ as the head. Jesus' message had focused on future events rather than recalling the first Passover. Now Jesus informed his disciples that one of them sitting at the table would betray him into the hands of his enemies.

It was not apparent which disciple it would be, and each disciple looked around the table hoping it would not be him. Jesus, though, knew exactly which one of his followers had turned away from God.

Jesus' role in God's plan of salvation had already been determined even before a Savior was promised to Adam and Eve. Judas' betrayal was the devastating catalyst setting it all into motion. However, Judas himself made the decision to betray Jesus, and he was solely responsible for the turmoil that his deception would eventually cause within his own soul.

- What emotions surface when you consider the betrayal of Jesus?
- Can you think of a time when your actions led to hurtful consequences?

Prayer Prompt: Thank God for his unending grace in your times of weakness.

# *Who Is the Greatest?*

❖

**Jesus said to them, "The kings of the Gentiles lord it over them; and those who exercise authority over them call themselves Benefactors. But you are not to be like that. Instead, the greatest among you should be like the youngest, and the one who rules like the one who serves."**

LUKE 22:25-26 NIV

The pressure of not knowing which man would betray Jesus caused an argument to break out at the dinner table about who was the greatest disciple.

Jesus did not settle this debate but, rather, quickly pointed out that true disciples do not follow the ways of the world. Society is concerned about position and power, but in the family of believers, no time should be spent assigning status or determining rank.

To be a benefactor is to give aid to someone in a lower position. Though Jesus has been given all authority over heaven and earth, he is much more than a benefactor. He didn't just give aid—he gave everything he had! He gave his life so the least among us could reign in his kingdom forever.

Looking forward to eternity, we can humbly serve others and put their needs ahead of our own, knowing it is truly Jesus we are serving.

- In what ways does society admire position and power?
- What could it look like to serve others before ourselves?

Prayer Prompt: Ask Jesus to give you a servant's heart.

# *Jesus Predicts Peter's Denial*

❖

**"Simon, Simon, Satan has asked to sift all of you as wheat. But I have prayed for you, Simon, that your faith may not fail. And when you have turned back, strengthen your brothers." But he replied, "Lord, I am ready to go with you to prison and to death." Jesus answered, "I tell you, Peter, before the rooster crows today, you will deny three times that you know me."**
**Luke 22:31-34 NIV**

Although Jesus had given instruction and authority to all his disciples, he specifically turned his attention to Simon Peter, their outspoken representative. Displaying his omniscience as God the Son, Jesus revealed that Satan had asked for access to the Twelve. It is only through the mediation of Jesus' prayers that the disciples could withstand such an attack from the devil.

Here Jesus also foretold that Peter would fall into sin, but when Peter realized his sin, he would repent and then be called to lead the other disciples. Though Peter could not imagine such a scenario, Jesus very pointedly told him what his sin would look like.

The disciples had no idea what the night would bring, but Jesus was making it very clear that he knew exactly what would happen. He was not going to be a helpless victim but, rather, a willing sacrifice.

- How could it help the disciples to hear these predictions?
- What does it mean to you that Jesus mediates for you?

Prayer Prompt: Praise Jesus for being your mediator.

# Jesus Prays in the Garden

**"Father, if you are willing, take this cup from me; yet not my will, but yours be done." An angel from heaven appeared to him and strengthened him. And being in anguish, he prayed more earnestly, and his sweat was like drops of blood falling to the ground.**

LUKE 22:42-44 NIV

After God created the world, there was a man in a garden with a tree. The sin this man committed would ruin every corner of the world, yet God promised that despite the man's failure to obey, God would one day restore him to complete perfection.

On this night, there was a man in a garden praying earnestly and preparing for death by way of a tree. This man had obeyed God's every command perfectly, yet God promised that if this man continued to obey, he would be punished and forsaken by God. As a result, every corner of the world would be restored.

As Jesus approached the completion of God's salvation, he prayed for strength. Usually after times of quiet prayer, Jesus was refreshed and ready to continue. Here an angel strengthened him, and still he prayed with anguish in his soul. The heaviness of the burden he was to carry to the cross was being revealed to him. The cup he bore was God's wrath.

- What was the anguish Jesus experienced?
- What comfort can we find in Jesus' hour of prayer?

Prayer Prompt: Thank God for a Savior who understands deep grief.

# Even in Darkness

**"This is your hour—when darkness reigns."**

LUKE 22:53 NIV

Some days are just dark. Growing up, my family and I used to refer to these types of days as "stupid days." They were days where nothing went right, chaos ruled, and no matter how hard I tried to stay positive, I'd end the day drowning my sorrows in a massive bowl of mac and cheese.

Every time I read the account of Jesus' arrest, I can't help but think about what a "stupid day" it was for him. One of his closest friends betrayed him, and if that weren't bad enough, he did it with a sign of affection. Another friend chopped off someone's ear in an impulsive yet well-meaning moment of fear. And then Jesus was arrested for crimes he didn't commit.

This wasn't even a full day. These events probably all happened in what seemed like a blink. Jesus pointed out that they could've happened at any time on any day. He called this moment the hour "when darkness reigns." What a powerful statement in so many ways.

But Jesus didn't run away from the darkness. He responded to betrayal gently. He healed an injury patiently. Even in darkness, he loved.

- What darkness seems to be attacking your day today?
- How can you respond with love in this darkness?

Prayer prompt: Praise God for his incredible ability to love even in the darkest of moments.

# Peter, the Man of Extremes

❖

**A servant girl saw [Peter] sitting near the light.**
**She looked closely at him and said,**
**"This man also was with him."**
**But he denied it, saying, "Woman, I do not know him."**
LUKE 22:56-57 EHV

Peter's emotions must have run the gamut in the hours before Jesus was crucified.

The Lord had just strengthened the disciples with his body and blood—and had given a new promise of forgiveness. Soon after, Jesus was arrested, and Peter attacked the high priest's servant, cutting off his ear. Now, in the courtyard of the high priest, a girl identifies Peter, but his bloody weapon remains sheathed.

How could Peter have had the courage to swing a sword at an official's head but then cower at the accusation of a girl? Sadly, I know.

With Jesus at my side, I have acted boldly to defend the honor of my Savior. And in the darkness of temptation, I have succumbed to fear and chosen sin. How I ache over my sin! Like Peter, I can fiercely love Christ in one moment and deny him in another. I am humbled with Peter in my unfaithfulness to Christ. Again. And again. And again.

Jesus would suffer and die to pay for my sins. I am forgiven through his blood.

- How does the humiliation of our sin prepare our hearts for his forgiveness?
- Think of times when you are afraid to confess Christ.

Prayer Prompt: Confess your unfaithfulness to Christ. Ask for forgiveness.

# He Looks at Me

❖

**At that very moment, . . . the rooster crowed. The Lord turned and looked at Peter. Then Peter remembered the Lord's word, how he had said to him, "Before the rooster crows today you will deny me three times."**

LUKE 22:60-61 EHV

I think of the gamut of emotions Jesus may have felt. The joy of the Passover meal and the bitterness of betrayal. The disappointment in the garden and the fear of crucifixion's brutality. But Jesus always keeps the needs of others in mind. Though his crucifixion was imminent, Jesus extended forgiveness to Peter, his beloved follower.

And he also extends it to me.

I have imagined the look in Jesus' eyes a thousand times, not thinking of Peter but thinking about me. I need my Savior's look of forgiveness because I know my sin. I am desperate for his love and grace—and completely unworthy.

Yet I receive the look, the love, the sacrifice, and the forgiveness. I see Jesus' eyes every time I read the Word, receive his Supper, or remember my baptism.

He looks at me.

I cannot rely on the strength or intentions of my faith because it fails. I trust only in the forgiveness given by my Savior. My repentance is met with love. I am forgiven.

- What are some times you have received this look?
- Can you tell others about how Jesus looks at them?

Prayer Prompt: Praise Jesus for turning his head and looking at you again and again.

# The Jewish Judgment

**"If you are the Christ, tell us."**
**But [Jesus] said to them, "If I tell you, you will not believe."**
**So they all said, "Are you the Son of God, then?"**
**And he said to them, "You say that I am."**

LUKE 22:67,70 ESV

After Jesus' arrest late that Holy Thursday, he was taken to the Jewish council for questioning. Annas and his son-in-law Caiaphas ruled the Jewish council as high priests.

They needed to find a charge against Jesus that would result in a conviction, but the question that fueled their hatred was "Are you the Son of God?"

Jesus' reply reflected the insincerity of the conversation. He knew their hearts.

The Jews saw Jesus' miracles and healings. They heard his teachings, prayers, and wisdom, but they rejected Jesus. Their hearts were hard.

Jesus is still rejected by hard hearts today. Yet we boldly proclaim the Son of God, crucified to pay for sin and resurrected as proof that our salvation is secure. When Jesus returns, all people will know he is the Son of God. On that day, may he see your heart of faith and joyfully acknowledge, "You say that I am!"

- What blessings do you have by faith in Jesus as the Son of God?
- How does Jesus' response help you when people just want to argue about religion?

Prayer Prompt: Praise God for Jesus' willingness to go to the cross for our sin.

# Pilate Questions Jesus

**Pilate asked Jesus, "Are you the king of the Jews?"**
**"You have said so," Jesus replied.**

LUKE 23:3 NIV

The Jews brought Jesus to Pilate early Friday morning. The Romans were known for public trials with quick, brutal dispatches of justice. That's exactly what the Jewish leaders wanted. They needed Rome to crucify him expeditiously.

The Jews brought charges that got Pilate's attention: "We have found this man subverting our nation. He opposes payment of taxes to Caesar and claims to be Messiah, a king" (Luke 23:2). They had *found* their verdict and needed Pilate's rubber stamp to be rid of Jesus.

Pilate asked Jesus if he was the king of the Jews. Jesus' answer, "You have said so," confirmed what Pilate already knew: "No basis for a charge" (Luke 23:4).

An outcry from the Jews followed. When Pilate heard that Jesus had started preaching in Galilee, he saw an escape for himself. Herod ruled Galilee and happened to be in town, so Pilate sent Jesus to Herod.

Through all of this, Jesus didn't argue against the false charges. He wasn't afraid of Rome's injustice. He knew there would be a day of final, faultless judgment before God. He would stand on judgment day with perfect, kingly justice and declare us not guilty because of his sacrifice.

- Why didn't the Jews bring charges of blasphemy?
- Why might we say that we both long for and dread God's perfect justice?

Prayer Prompt: Praise Jesus, your King and judge.

# Jesus Before Herod

❖

**[Herod] questioned [Jesus] at some length, but he made no answer. The chief priests and the scribes stood by, vehemently accusing him. And Herod with his soldiers treated him with contempt and mocked him. Then . . . he sent him back to Pilate.**

LUKE 23:9-11 ESV

Herod Antipas was the leader who demanded the head of John the Baptist on a platter. He was an evil man like his father, Herod the Great, who slaughtered many baby boys after Jesus' birth.

As millions of Jews gathered in Jerusalem, Herod, like Pilate, was in the city as a show of power to the masses. Pilate sent Jesus to the palace where Herod was staying. Herod hoped Jesus would perform a miracle, but Jesus' miracles weren't for show. Herod hounded Jesus with questions, but Jesus remained silent. It was a searing rebuke to Herod.

The mockery resumed as the Jewish accusers watched. Then Herod sent Jesus back to Pilate to be condemned and crucified.

But Jesus' innocent suffering and death didn't happen because of Rome's power. Jesus willingly went to the cross of his own free will to pay for sin. Jesus died because he loves you.

- What does this thirst for cruelty tell you about the depth of sin?
- Why do you think Jesus remained silent before Herod?

Prayer Prompt: Ask God to bind the hands of evildoers.

# With One Voice

**They all shouted together with one voice: "Take him away!"**
LUKE 23:18 EHV

Jesus returned to Pilate, and for the second time, Pilate told the crowds that Jesus was innocent.

"With one voice," the Jews cried out for Jesus' condemnation. The chief priests had stirred up the crowds, and no one dissented from the evil plan that gripped the hearts of Jesus' accusers. Bound in hate, the people demanded the crucifixion of God's promised Messiah. In unison, they echoed the murderous heart and voice of Satan. Their sin was ripe and brought a harvest of death.

Without the grace of Christ, my voice would have joined the chant to kill the Savior. If not for God's mercy I would stand eternally condemned, shaking my fist at the heavens.

His blood is on my hands.

Amid the shouts of hate, Jesus went to the cross to pay for sin. The crowds may have shouted for Jesus to be taken away, but it was his own merciful love and willing obedience to God that sent him to the cross. Jesus chose to be the Lamb of God that would take away the sin of the world.

"He humbled himself by becoming obedient to death—even death on a cross!" (Philippians 2:8 NIV).

- How do you give voice to your faith?
- Which people support your voice of faith, and how do you support others?

Prayer Prompt: Confess that your voice has not been united with the truth and love of God.

# Blinded to the Lamb of God

**Wanting to release Jesus, Pilate appealed to them again. But they kept shouting, "Crucify him! Crucify him!"**

LUKE 23:20-21 NIV

Three times Jesus had been declared innocent, yet Pilate's appeal to release Jesus was a paltry effort. He saw through the false charges and schemes of the Jews, but he acted like a puppet. What Roman authority had ever been manipulated so completely?

The Jews closed in for the kill. The scent of suffering made their pious blood run wild. What riled them to such a passion for torture? How could they look past Jesus' innocence to accuse him with lies? How could they reject his love and cry out for his crucifixion?

Sin blinded them from seeing the Lamb of God. Their guilt is appalling.

So is mine.

I don't shout "Crucify him!" when I sin, but I look past Jesus and choose evil. His suffering does not always deter my selfishness. His gentleness does not always calm my lust. His mercy does not always lessen my pride. I look past his bloody robes, dismissing the white robe of righteousness he offers. This is the nature of sin.

Yet Jesus willingly paid my debt.

- Why does it help you to remember your sin and Jesus' suffering?
- How does blindness to Jesus' mercy help you understand the unbelievers around you?

Prayer Prompt: Ask God to open the eyes of the blind. Thank God that he may work through you to open their eyes.

# The Request Is Decreed

❖

**With loud shouts they insistently demanded that he be crucified, and their shouts prevailed. So Pilate decided to grant their demand . . . and surrendered Jesus to their will.**

LUKE 23:23-25 NIV

Pilate had Jesus flogged in hopes that it would subdue the raging crowd. The scourging included brutal blows with a spiked whip to bring Jesus to the brink of death. The Jews didn't care. They just wanted Jesus dead and his message silenced. Hatred overpowered Rome's justice. Never underestimate the power of evil.

After repeatedly declaring Jesus' innocence, Pilate surrendered to the Jewish demands. He stated no charge against Jesus but delivered a sentence of death by crucifixion. Pilate may have washed his hands to symbolize his own innocence (Matthew 27:24), but he commanded his soldiers to crucify our sinless Savior.

The punishment was enforced immediately.

We know Pilate decreed Jesus' crucifixion. Pilate surrendered to the will of the Jews who were consumed with hatred. At the same time, we know that our sin caused Jesus to suffer and die. God had a plan to save the world. Jesus himself had surrendered to that plan hours earlier when he declared, "Not my will, but yours be done" (Luke 22:42).

- Think about all who contributed to Pilate's dilemma and decision.
- Why do we blame Pilate when it was Jesus who chose to go to the cross?

Prayer Prompt: Confess your sins, knowing Jesus willingly went to the cross to pay for them all.

# *King of the Jews*

❖

**There was a written notice above him, which read:**

**THIS IS THE KING OF THE JEWS.**

LUKE 23:38 NIV

As if the beatings, public mocking, and shameful humiliation of the crucifixion weren't enough, Pilate installed a written notice above the cross of Jesus. Such notices displayed the crime that had been committed, and Pilate was very intentional about what he wrote. The notice was written in Greek, Latin, and Aramaic (similar to Hebrew) so everyone could read it (John 19:20).

The ironic notice was meant to mock and humiliate Jesus. The Jews objected, saying Jesus merely "claimed to be king of the Jews" (John 19:21), and the soldiers taunted, "If you are the king of the Jews, save yourself" (Luke 23:37). A man hanging on a cross is certainly no worthy king.

But the double irony of the situation contained truth. Jesus is the King of the Jews! He's also the King of the Gentiles, the King of all. And his work of salvation, his conquering victory, would soon be complete.

Today, many languages proclaim Jesus as the Savior and Lord of all people. He is truly the King of kings!

- Explain how love is the universal language through which we can share Jesus with others.
- When is it hard to accept that Jesus is the Savior for all people?

Prayer Prompt: Praise Jesus, your conquering King who endured the suffering of the cross so you could join him in his kingdom.

# Jesus, Remember Me

❖

**Then [the one criminal] said, "Jesus, remember me when you come into your kingdom." Jesus answered him, "Truly I tell you, today you will be with me in paradise."**

LUKE 23:42-43 NIV

Despite enduring the same Roman punishment, one criminal beside Jesus still had strength to hurl insults at him. He had no faith that Jesus could truly save him. But in an unexpected turn of events, the other criminal receives salvation. He boldly states that Jesus is innocent and believes him to be the Messiah who can save him.

What faith from this man! Knowing the end is soon approaching, he utters a bold prayer. It's no small request: he asks to be remembered and received into Jesus' kingdom. This criminal saw beyond his present circumstance to the coming glory that was near.

Jesus' answer is a personal assurance of salvation to that repentant sinner. Even in the darkest moment, the gospel triumphs over all human weakness.

On the cross, Jesus remembered a totally undeserving thief. For you, he offers that same assurance and enters his kingdom so that you might enter it too.

- How can you boldly pray to your Savior?
- What comfort can we take from Jesus' answer when we suffer in this life?

Prayer Prompt: Ask God for boldness in prayer. Thank God that the suffering on earth will be followed by paradise in heaven.

# The Temple Curtain Tears

❖

**It was now about noon, and darkness came over the whole land until three in the afternoon, for the sun stopped shining. And the curtain of the temple was torn in two.**

LUKE 23:44-45 NIV

Can you imagine what it was like for complete darkness to cover the land for three hours in the middle of the day? All nature seemed to mourn the suffering of God's Son. The Light of the world was extinguished.

When Jesus died, the curtain in the Most Holy Place of God's temple was torn in two. The barrier of the curtain separated sinful people from their holy God. In the Old Testament, God designed this holy place to hold the ark of the covenant. The Jews were instructed to celebrate the Passover every year by sending a priest into the Most Holy Place to sprinkle blood on the ark's mercy seat to atone for sin.

At Jesus' death, the symbolic barrier between God and humanity was torn in two. The torn curtain symbolized that Christ's work on the cross was complete. "He has appeared once for all . . . to do away with sin by the sacrifice of himself" (Hebrews 9:26).

Now you and all people can approach God through Christ.

- How does the temple curtain tearing help you understand Jesus' role as High Priest?
- How might the Jews have felt when the curtain tore?

Prayer Prompt: Praise God that you can now approach him because of Jesus' sacrifice on the cross.

# A Proper Burial

❖

**Going to Pilate, [Joseph] asked for Jesus' body. Then he took it down, wrapped it in linen cloth and placed it in a tomb cut in the rock, one in which no one had yet been laid.**

LUKE 23:52-53 NIV

At the foot of the cross, many people watched the death of their Savior and could do nothing. After Jesus died, we see an unlikely man boldly step forward to honor his Lord.

Joseph of Arimathea was a prominent figure in Jewish circles who was "waiting for the kingdom of God" (Luke 23:51). He was respected enough to have Pilate grant his request, and his love for Jesus prompted him to ask for his Savior's body to give him a proper burial.

His actions are a beautiful example of devotion. Joseph responded in faith and grasped the opportunity to serve Jesus despite any consequences it may have caused him.

As believers, we may feel like we can't do much for Jesus, but we are called to take advantage of the opportunities given to us, doing what we can out of thankfulness for what our Savior has done for us. His death paid for our sins, and his love compels us to live in gratitude.

- How can you profess your faith more boldly?
- What resources and abilities can you use to serve others out of love for Christ?

Prayer Prompt: Confess the times when you didn't stand up for Jesus. Ask God for boldness to share your faith.

# He Is Raised

❖

**"Why are you looking for the living among the dead? He is not here, but has been raised!"**

LUKE 24:5-6 EHV

Where can Jesus be found? Not in a cemetery, but among the living and in his Word, in his own teachings about himself. This was true on that first Easter morning, and it is true today. The women who went to the tomb that morning expected to find the dead body of their dear friend and teacher, Jesus. What they found were angels who questioned them: "Why? Why look here?"

The angels continued, "Remember how he told you while he was still in Galilee that the Son of Man must be delivered over to the hands of sinful men, and be crucified, and the third day rise again?" (Luke 24:6-7). Maybe the women had forgotten Jesus' words because the laws of nature say that dead people stay dead. But at the angels' words, the women did remember and believe. We can trust God's Word just as these women could. We can believe Jesus is alive, despite the laws of nature, because the Bible says so and God always keeps his promises.

- Are there promises of God you struggle to believe because the laws of nature say they can't be so?
- How can you look for Jesus among the living?

Prayer Prompt: Thank Jesus for telling us who he is and where we can find him.

# Run to See

**Peter got up and ran to the tomb. Bending over to look in, he saw only the strips of linen cloth. He went home, amazed at what had happened.**

LUKE 24:12 EHV

Has your word ever been doubted? When Mary Magdalene, Joanna, Mary the mother of James, and the other women told the disciples what they had seen and heard, the men thought it was "nonsense" (Luke 24:11). It's not surprising that the men didn't believe them. After all, Jesus was dead. How could he not be in the tomb?

But Peter ran to see. Could it be? Could the women be right? Maybe, as he was running, he was hoping to see Jesus or to meet the angels who had spoken to the women. Maybe he wanted to prove the women wrong. What he saw were just the burial cloths—no Jesus, no angels. He was "amazed," but he still did not understand.

Much of God's Word amazes us, and the good news we tell others about Jesus is often met with skepticism. It sounds like nonsense to unbelievers. Yet if we run to see as Peter did, we find an empty tomb and marvel even if we don't understand.

- How does it make you feel that women were the first to know about the resurrection?
- Are you ever afraid to talk about Jesus because someone might say it is nonsense?

Prayer Prompt: Ask the Holy Spirit to help you believe even the most amazing parts of Scripture.

# Burning Hearts

❖

**They said to each other, "Were not our hearts burning within us while he was speaking to us along the road and while he was explaining the Scriptures to us?"**

LUKE 24:32 EHV

A heart on fire, filled with love, longing, sorrow, and joy all at once? Is that what Cleopas and his companion felt as Jesus walked with them on the road to Emmaus? The crucifixion was still fresh in their minds, as was the news from the women that Jesus was not in the tomb. What could it mean?

The men didn't know they were talking to Jesus, and they told him all about the happenings in Jerusalem. Jesus' response might sound a bit harsh to us. He said they were being "foolish" (Luke 24:25), but then he explained everything. As always, he used Scripture to show them how all the prophecies had been fulfilled in his life, death, and resurrection. They were so interested in what he had to say—their hearts burning—that they asked him to stay for dinner. They wanted to hear more. Suddenly, they realized this man was Jesus. And just as suddenly, he was gone. They ran to tell the others all they had experienced.

- When has the study of Scripture caused your heart to burn?
- What prophecies about Jesus do you know?

Prayer Prompt: Thank God for the Scriptures concerning Jesus. Thank Jesus for his patience with and love for you. Ask for a burning heart that longs to hear about Jesus.

# Witnesses

**Then [Jesus] opened [the disciples'] minds
to understand the Scriptures.
He said to them, "This is what is written and so it must be:
The Christ will suffer and rise from the dead on the
third day, and repentance and forgiveness of sins
will be preached in his name to all nations."**

LUKE 24:45-47 EHV

After walking on the road to Emmaus with Cleopas and his companion, Jesus also appeared to his disciples. Though they were afraid, he reassured them, showed them the scars on his hands and feet, and asked them for food. He gently chided them for their doubts and their troubled hearts.

Finally, Jesus opened the disciples' minds, helping them understand all that had happened and would happen. He called them witnesses and promised to clothe them "with power from on high" (Luke 24:49). This power would be the Holy Spirit, who would come to help the disciples preach about Jesus. He also comes to us in Scripture to create faith in our hearts. Our minds are opened to trust in God's plan of salvation just as the minds of the disciples were opened. We have been preached to, and it is now our job to proclaim.

- Why do you think the disciples doubted?
- Do you think of yourself as a witness like the disciples? How can you be a witness?

Prayer Prompt: Praise God that your mind has been opened to Scripture and you have been "clothed with power from on high" (Luke 24:49).

# Jesus Ascends Into Heaven

❖

**While [Jesus] was blessing them, he parted from them and was taken up into heaven. So they worshipped him and returned to Jerusalem with great joy.**

LUKE 24:51-52 EHV

Joy, great joy! It was hard to say good-bye, but the disciples finally understood Jesus' mission and God's plan. What an amazing sight it must have been and what a sublime feeling to be blessed by Jesus himself and watch him rise into heaven, knowing that he will come back to take his brothers and sisters to be with him. They worshiped him for all he had done and all that he is. I can imagine it, I can almost see it, and by God's grace, I can believe it.

The disciples didn't stay there in Bethany looking up to the sky. They returned to Jerusalem and prepared to share the good news of the forgiveness of sins through Jesus with other people in need of joy.

Today, Christians sometimes experience moments of great joy and magnificence, but then they must go home like the disciples did. And the disciples are a good example of what to do next. Luke 24:53 says, "They were continually in the temple courts, praising and blessing God." May Jesus find us continually praising him when he returns!

- Recount for yourself a moment of great joy in your spiritual life.
- In what ways can you continually praise God?

Prayer Prompt: Worship Jesus for who he is and what he has done.

# Index


| PAGE | | |
|---|---|---|
| 7 | Luke **1:3–4** | Unfolding the Elaborate Plan |
| 11 | Luke **1:13–14** | Prophet of the Most High |
| 12 | Luke **1:26–27,31–32** | Son of the Most High |
| 13 | Luke **1:38** | May Your Word Be Fulfilled |
| 14 | Luke **1:46–47** | My Spirit Rejoices |
| 17 | Luke **2:1** | Enter, King Jesus! |
| 18 | Luke **2:8–11** | The Most Unique Announcement |
| 19 | Luke **2:11–12** | Seek and Find |
| 20 | Luke **2:13–15** | A Great Company |
| 21 | Luke **2:28,30–32** | Eyes of Faith |
| 22 | Luke **2:34–35** | A Sword Will Pierce Your Own Soul |
| 23 | Luke **2:38** | A Godly Widow |
| 24 | Luke **2:49,51** | Letting Go |
| 25 | Luke **2:52** | Growing |
| 29 | Luke **3:2–3** | John's Message |
| 30 | Luke **3:7–9** | Fruits of Repentance |
| 31 | Luke **3:16** | The Worthy One |
| 32 | Luke **3:21** | The Baptism of Jesus |
| 33 | Luke **3:21–22** | The Triune God |
| 34 | Luke **4:1–2** | Tempted for a Purpose |
| 35 | Luke **4:3–4** | Bread for the Soul |
| 36 | Luke **4:6–7** | The Temptation of Power |
| 37 | Luke **4:12** | Testing God |
| 38 | Luke **4:13** | The Devil Doesn't Give Up |
| 41 | Luke **4:18** | Do You Know What You're Doing? |
| 42 | Luke **4:21** | It Is Fulfilled |
| 43 | Luke **4:25,27** | Providence for the Pagan, Healing for the Heathen |
| 44 | Luke **4:43** | I Must |
| 45 | Luke **5:3–4** | Perfect Priorities |
| 46 | Luke **5:8** | Seeing Our Sin |
| 47 | Luke **5:12** | Simple and Powerful Prayer |
| 48 | Luke **5:18–19** | Best Friends Forever |
| 49 | Luke **5:23–24** | He's the Real Deal |
| 50 | Luke **5:27–28** | He Sees You |

# Index


| PAGE | | |
|---|---|---|
| 51 | Luke **5:31-32** | Help to Heal |
| 52 | Luke **5:33-34** | Full Forgiveness and Fellowship |
| 55 | Luke **6:21** | Hungry for More |
| 56 | Luke **6:38** | Be a Messy Chef |
| 57 | Luke **6:45** | Spiritual Marinade |
| 58 | Luke **7:2-5** | Gatekeeping God's Love |
| 59 | Luke **7:6-7,9** | Amazing Faith |
| 60 | Luke **7:20-22** | An Important Question |
| 61 | Luke **7:33-35** | Wisdom's Children |
| 62 | Luke **7:37-38,48,50** | Overwhelmed by Gratitude |
| 63 | Luke **8:5** | Just Scatter |
| 64 | Luke **8:15** | A Farmer's Guide to Soul Care |
| 65 | Luke **8:16** | On a Stand |
| 66 | Luke **8:21** | We Are Family |
| 69 | Luke **9:17** | Feeding of the Five Thousand |
| 70 | Luke **9:18-20** | Who Do You Say I Am? |
| 71 | Luke **9:23** | Give Up Your Own Way |
| 72 | Luke **9:29-31** | The Glory of Jesus |
| 73 | Luke **9:35** | This Is My Son, My Chosen One |
| 74 | Luke **9:44-45** | They Didn't Understand |
| 75 | Luke **9:49-50** | Anyone Not Against Us |
| 76 | Luke **9:57-58,60,62** | Discipleship |
| 77 | Luke **10:21** | What Brings You Joy? |
| 78 | Luke **10:23** | Don't Miss That! |
| 79 | Luke **10:24** | What Is to Come |
| 80 | Luke **10:30** | The Bad Guys |
| 81 | Luke **10:34-35** | Good Story, Good Guy |
| 82 | Luke **10:38** | Come In! |
| 83 | Luke **10:39-40** | Don't You Care? |
| 84 | Luke **10:41-42** | What One Thing? |
| 85 | Luke **11:1** | The Need for Prayer |
| 86 | Luke **11:2** | Father |
| 87 | Luke **11:3** | All Our Needs |
| 88 | Luke **11:4** | Deliver Us |

## Index


| PAGE | | |
|---|---|---|
| 91 | Luke **11:29** | Do You Need a Sign? |
| 92 | Luke **11:33** | Is Your Flashlight On? |
| 93 | Luke **11:34** | Bad Eyes |
| 94 | Luke **11:39** | Dirty Dishes |
| 97 | Luke **12:6-7** | What Are You Really Worth? |
| 98 | Luke **12:18-20** | Know Any Rich Fools? |
| 99 | Luke **12:27-28** | The Kadupul Blossom |
| 100 | Luke **12:37** | Be Watchful |
| 101 | Luke **12:51** | Christ Alone |
| 102 | Luke **13:2-3** | Asking the Best Question |
| 103 | Luke **13:12-13** | Free to Praise |
| 104 | Luke **13:15-16** | Free to Rest |
| 105 | Luke **13:20-21** | Yeast |
| 106 | Luke **13:24** | Narrow Door |
| 107 | Luke **13:29** | People Will Come |
| 108 | Luke **13:34** | I Longed to Gather You |
| 109 | Luke **14:11** | He Who Humbles Himself |
| 110 | Luke **14:16-18** | Declining the Greatest Invitation |
| 111 | Luke **14:23-24** | Attending the Great Banquet |
| 112 | Luke **14:25-27** | The Real Cost |
| 113 | Luke **14:28** | Building Expenses |
| 114 | Luke **14:31** | Waging War and Winning |
| 115 | Luke **14:34-35** | That's Gross |
| 116 | Luke **15:4** | Greener Pastures |
| 117 | Luke **15:8-9** | A Reason to Rejoice |
| 118 | Luke **15:24** | The Prodigal Son |
| 119 | Luke **15:25,28** | The Other Prodigal Son |
| 120 | Luke **15:31-32** | The Father's Love |
| 121 | Luke **16:10** | The Check Mark of Faithfulness |
| 122 | Luke **16:13** | Why God Is Our Master |
| 123 | Luke **16:25** | He Is Comforted |
| 124 | Luke **16:27-28,31** | Let Them Listen |
| 125 | Luke **17:1** | Protect Others From Stumbling |
| 126 | Luke **17:3** | Forgiveness Restores |

# Index


| PAGE | | |
|---|---|---|
| 127 | Luke **17:5-6** | Faith Like a Mustard Seed |
| 128 | Luke **17:10** | Take Up Your Duty With Joy |
| 129 | Luke **17:15-16** | Ten Lepers |
| 130 | Luke **17:30-33** | When Jesus Appears |
| 131 | Luke **18:1** | The Persistent Widow |
| 132 | Luke **18:14** | The Pharisee and the Tax Collector |
| 133 | Luke **18:16** | Such as These |
| 134 | Luke **18:18** | Who Can Be Saved? |
| 137 | Luke **18:31-33** | Everything Written |
| 138 | Luke **18:39-42** | Sight for the Man of Faith |
| 139 | Luke **19:8-10** | Zacchaeus |
| 140 | Luke **19:12-13** | The Minas Are Given |
| 141 | Luke **19:16-21** | The Minas Accounted For |
| 142 | Luke **19:31** | The Lord Needs It |
| 143 | Luke **19:40** | A Stone's Cry |
| 144 | Luke **19:41-42** | Jerusalem Moments |
| 145 | Luke **19:46** | A Different Kind of Mad |
| 146 | Luke **20:2** | Whose Authority? |
| 147 | Luke **20:9-10** | The Evil Tenants |
| 148 | Luke **20:13-16** | The Son Is Sent |
| 149 | Luke **20:22** | What's the Real Question? |
| 150 | Luke **20:34-35** | The Age to Come |
| 151 | Luke **20:41** | True God and True Man |
| 152 | Luke **20:46** | A New Robe |
| 153 | Luke **21:2-4** | Quality, Not Quantity |
| 154 | Luke **21:8-9** | Do Not Be Terrified |
| 155 | Luke **21:15** | I Will Give You Words |
| 156 | Luke **21:28** | Lift Up Your Heads |
| 157 | Luke **21:34** | Watch Yourselves |
| 158 | Luke **22:3-6** | Judas Succumbs |
| 159 | Luke **22:8,10-12** | Preparations for the Passover |
| 160 | Luke **22:15-16** | Jesus' Eager Desire |
| 161 | Luke **22:19-20** | Jesus Institutes the Lord's Supper |
| 162 | Luke **22:21-22** | A Passover Like No Other |
| 163 | Luke **22:25-26** | Who Is the Greatest? |

## Index


| PAGE | | |
|---|---|---|
| 164 | Luke **22:31-34** | Jesus Predicts Peter's Denial |
| 165 | Luke **22:42-44** | Jesus Prays in the Garden |
| 166 | Luke **22:53** | Even in Darkness |
| 167 | Luke **22:56-57** | Peter, the Man of Extremes |
| 168 | Luke **22:60-61** | He Looks at Me |
| 169 | Luke **22:67,70** | The Jewish Judgment |
| 170 | Luke **23:3** | Pilate Questions Jesus |
| 171 | Luke **23:9-11** | Jesus Before Herod |
| 172 | Luke **23:18** | With One Voice |
| 173 | Luke **23:20-21** | Blinded to the Lamb of God |
| 174 | Luke **23:23-25** | The Request Is Decreed |
| 175 | Luke **23:38** | King of the Jews |
| 176 | Luke **23:42-43** | Jesus, Remember Me |
| 177 | Luke **23:44-45** | The Temple Curtain Tears |
| 178 | Luke **23:52-53** | A Proper Burial |
| 179 | Luke **24:5-6** | He Is Raised |
| 180 | Luke **24:12** | Run to See |
| 181 | Luke **24:32** | Burning Hearts |
| 182 | Luke **24:45-47** | Witnesses |
| 183 | Luke **24:51-52** | Jesus Ascends Into Heaven |